Everything is a Big Deal, Until It's Not

Laurie Condon

Black Rose Writing | Texas

First printing

Some names and identifying details may have been changed to protect the privacy of individuals.

ISBN: 978-1-68433-376-9
PUBLISHED BY BLACK ROSE WRITING
www.blackrosewriting.com

Printed in the United States of America
Suggested Retail Price (SRP) $16.95

Everything is a Big Deal, Until It's Not is printed in Calluna

For Superman,
My first, My last, My Everything.

Everything is a Big Deal, Until It's Not

CONTENTS

INTRODUCTION

I can remember being a kid anticipating all of the milestones I could not wait to hit and watching my sister, who is ten years older than I am, get there first.

I always thought she was so cool, so I wanted to participate in whatever she was doing.

Things have changed now. I do not really envy her menopause, and frankly, I thought that I was going to miss that period (pun intended) because of the active lifestyle I lead.

So, as I sit here reflecting and trying to figure out a way to embrace the unknown rather than worry about it, I cannot help but realize that many good things come out of the hard times. It is recognizing the good that is paramount to making the most of the journey.

This is a trip down memory lane for me. I have been trying to take inventory of where I am and how I got to this place. What prompted this nostalgia was my own experience with peri-menopause. Prior to peri-menopause, I never really thought too much about how old I was because I have always felt much younger than my age. However, when my period started getting erratic, and my weight started going up for no good reason, it dawned on me that it had arrived. Aside from the physical symptoms, I am experiencing, I cannot stop thinking about being old. I know age is just a number, but honestly, I have reached a high number, and I am not jazzed. So, the revelation that Everything Is A Big Deal Until It Is Not dawned on me when I was thinking about how much getting older sucks. I started remembering that puberty was not much fun either, nor was dating, nor doing term papers, interviewing for jobs, etc. Hence the title. I just want to be mindful of all of the many accomplishments and lessons I have learned and keep enjoying life to its fullest potential.

PUBERTY

"ARE YOU THERE GOD?"

From the fourth grade on, I was enamored with every adolescent book written by Judy Blume. Her novels gave me a peek into the unchartered waters of puberty. By the time I started to notice my body changing, I was vigilantly doing my daily "we must, we must, we must increase our bust" exercises I garnered from *Are You There God, It's Me Margaret.*

I was right on schedule and got my first period at age twelve and a half. When my breasts started developing, my mom suggested we go shopping for a bra. I still cannot adjust the straps without help, and this moment is one of the many times I realize how much I miss her. Puberty proved to be exciting, anxiety-provoking, and embarrassing. Embarrassing simply because these types of topics were not talked about in my house. Of course, we were encouraged to talk about anything we wanted, but the tension I would feel suggested otherwise. Similarly, the ten- year age difference between my sister and I precluded this type of discussion as well. She was already married and out of the house. Not to worry, I still had encyclopedia Judy Blume.

For the first time ever, I no longer needed to be threatened into taking a shower. Some people go through the notorious teenage awkward phase worse than others, and I was no exception. Between ages twelve and thirteen, I was chubby, had a protruding bite, and my mom made my clothes. I know, it sucked. I still cringe when I see Joan Cusack in *Sixteen Candles* drinking from the water fountain wearing her headgear. Thankfully I only had to wear my headgear at night. I was not on track to be voted prom queen, but for whatever reason, I was not aware of just how awkward I was even when I was in the throes of it. I attribute this to my parents, who instilled some sort of confidence in me and also to the fact that I always had friends who liked and accepted me.

I remember calling my mother when I first spotted (pun intended) the onset of my menstrual cycle. She was at work, and I was a little bit freaked out. I think some of my friends had already gotten their periods, so I knew it was coming, but I still recall feeling different after it officially started. Although I had several close friends, pubic hair and bras were difficult topics to bring up, which is why the Judy Blume reference guide normalized the uncertainty about what was happening for me. I recall those poor girls who were made fun of for being well endowed and subsequently accused of being easy for that reason. They were struggling with the same fears as other girls their age. Only a couple of years later they became the envy of their classmates, especially for the late bloomers.

This was the first time my weight became of interest to me. My baby fat was no longer cute, nor was I a baby. I was a woman (barely), and the stakes of adolescence were higher, so I was determined to lose weight. I sought out help from my mother, but she was hesitant to help me because my sister had just recovered from anorexia. With no other choice, I decided to take my weight into my own hands.

THE WEIGHT OF THE WORLD

When I was eight, I shadowed my sister and nagged her to let me tag along on her dates. I wanted to be included in her life. I could not reconcile the fact that she was not equally enthusiastic by the prospect of bringing me with her (skip ahead thirty-five years, it is like how I cannot understand why my son does not want me tagging along with him either). Granted I get it now, she was eighteen, and I do have some remorse about nagging her, but she was so mean about it, that years later we decided to call our actions a draw for all intents and purposes. However, on one occasion she extended a rare invite for me to accompany her and her boyfriend to a work picnic. I was so excited, I vowed that I was not going to be any trouble so that this invite would not be an anomaly. The significance of this outing changed the course of my entire adolescence.

We got to the picnic, and I went off on my own to swim in the lake while she hung around her colleagues and socialized. One of her co-workers, who seemed so much older, but was probably only eighteen, started talking to me. We were in the middle of the lake, and I began to feel uneasy. I did my best to get away, but it was only after he inappropriately touched me that I managed to escape. This event left me with a lot of uncomfortable feelings. I was too scared to tell my sister about what happened because I thought I would never be included again. So, I kept the incident to myself. Funny, when I try to remember the details, I cannot, but I can visualize the bathing suit I was wearing, and I can picture the gathering around the picnic tables after I had gotten free.

That evening I was so upset that I went into my parent's bedroom and I told my mother what had happened. I can still remember crawling into her bed, and I can even recall the quilt. I remember how hard it was to muster up the courage to tell her what had happened. I do not blame her at all, but she was ill-equipped to address what transpired, and we just swept it under the carpet.

This incident stayed in the recesses of my mind until it manifested itself into a full-fledged eating disorder. This may or may not have happened anyway, considering I wanted to lose weight, and both of my siblings had issues with anorexia previously, but this was the catalyst that propelled me into high gear. It certainly gave me something to focus on other than what had happened. The first five pounds melted off in a week. Suddenly I had laser beam focus. In addition to my new weight loss goal, I was determined to get myself onto the honor roll. I was going to be the best at everything I did. The more restrictions I put on myself, the better the results. I discovered the gym, and that expedited my weight loss. I could see the fruits of my effort and befriended anyone who shared a similar interest. We plotted different ways to diet and climb the social ladder, which was also becoming increasingly important. Even when I should not have had a care in the world, cruising around with my best friend in her Z300 with the T-tops off, smoking More cigarettes, listening to Lime and other Studio 54 classics, I had the added burden of being perfect.

I struggled every single day to avoid situations where I would have to face the temptation of fattening teenager friendly food. Now a foodie, I do not know how I managed. I existed on fumes for more than a decade. Although I did have friends who shared their desire to shed pounds, they were not as determined. They could turn their discipline on and off, but I only seemed to have one gear. At the time, I considered myself superior for being so committed, but when I think back, it makes me sad that I gave up all the food that is part of being a kid.

Time went on, and I started to get taller, and the weight kept dropping. When I entered ninth grade, I was eighty-nine pounds at five-foot-five-inches tall. By then, it was not that I thought I looked fat, but I was not happy, and dieting was something I was good at. When people told me, I was getting too thin, I automatically assumed they were jealous, and I cut them out of my life. I could not comprehend that there was such a thing as being too thin.

STARVING TO BE PERFECT

The recovery from anorexia is complex for several reasons. You cannot stop eating cold turkey, so you must get to the root of the issue. Studies show anorexia consistently happens to Type A personalities. As a driven person, abandoning anything, even unhealthy habits adds guilt to the equation. It feels like you have failed, and I really did not want to fail. An eating disorder is a full-time job. It allowed me to avoid thinking about dating and the unknowns, including sex. Being inappropriately touched at eight-years-old dampened my interest in boys, and I was perfectly happy to avoid engaging with the opposite sex for as long as I could rationalize.

My recovery from anorexia was not consistent until I met my husband. I give him a lot of credit for helping me finally overcome my demons. I had many successes but then slips. Those slips could be triggered by a situation or a relationship that caused me to regress. When I met my husband, he made me realize that when you are with someone who truly and unconditionally loves you, you are allowed to make mistakes. The chore of counting every calorie and being so rigid started to be less important. I wanted to focus on nurturing my relationship.

Will I ever not judge myself? Of course not, but I am more forgiving and less self-absorbed now. When I start to have those self-defeating thoughts, I try to change the conversation going on in my head. I reflect on all of my blessings and remind myself of my good fortune. I recognize there are things I can control, and for those I cannot, I can shut down the negative talk. As I stated, I was really scared to start dating but imagined that one day I would get married and have a family, so I realized I had to overcome my fear of intimacy.

YOU HAVE TO KISS A LOT OF FROGS

Many little girls play house and imagine their future fairytale family, with the handsome husband, the two kids, the white picket fence, and the dog. I had these visions too, but there was no dog, because of my Type A personality. I knew having a pet threatened the cleanliness of my abode, and I knew that the dog would cause me anxiety. These were safe fantasies. I did really want them to be my reality at some point, but because I was violated at such a young age, I struggled with my fear of engaging with the opposite sex, and I had not yet learned how to overcome these feelings. I had crushes and appreciated Shaun Cassidy, Rick Springfield and Andy Gibb no question. However, when I started to have feelings for boys in my classes, the butterflies were not only around the excitement but the recollection of how horrible it felt to be touched without permission.

This anxiety is why dieting was a crutch for me. I loved the fact that I continued to excel and supersede my goal, which was counterintuitive after a certain point. I was distracted and rationalized that I did not have to think about dating until I got to my ideal weight. That number changed every time I hit the goal I set, but by age fifteen, it was time for me to take the leap.

FIRST KISS

My best friend in high school was confident, energetic, and had no qualms about meeting guys and dating. I was a follower and fine with that. We were invited to many parties and spent several weekends out in New York City at South Street Seaport. One night, we went to a party, and I was talking to a guy, having the time of my life. He asked for my number, and I was ecstatic. I remember thinking he was totally out of my league. He was older, captain of the soccer team, and a Rock Star from where I was sitting.

A group of us made plans to hang out the following night at the beach. We got beers, which I know is illegal and I will deny to my son, but at the time it seemed perfectly legit. Later that night the Rock Star asked me to go for a walk on the beach alone. I was on cloud nine. I was wearing a sweater which I can still visualize down to the logo on my left breast. He was so smooth, and when we got away from the group, he expertly said, "oh you have something on your shirt (the logo)," and he copped a feel. I saw stars and checked French kiss off the list I kept in my head of things to do before I turned sixteen. It was so exciting for me, but I am sure when he realized just how inexperienced I was, he was over it immediately. To this day, I remember sitting in my parent's bedroom, on the rotary phone talking to him, scribbling our names in a heart.

FYI, I just stopped writing and Googled him. I could not find a picture, but I found several people that could be him. Why did I just waste hours looking for a picture when I would never reach out to him? I am just curious to see if he is as cute as I remember, or perhaps fat and bald, which is ultimately what I wish on all of my exes.

That experience with the Rock Star, although short-lived, gave me confidence. I was still in the throes of my eating issues which plagued every avenue of my life, but I had turned a corner. I was curious, and I was ready to experiment some more. Now, I really wanted a boyfriend, but there was a problem. How was I going to hide my eating issues? I was so focused on the number of calories I could consume on any given day and how much exercise I had to incorporate into my schedule, how could I fit in movies, social outings, and events where I did not know what mysterious food and drink would be offered that I would have to avoid. There was nothing carefree about me.

Many of my friends were consuming alcohol at this time, but being obsessed with calorie counting, I did not want the extra calories. I decided I had no other choice, but to smoke marijuana instead. Thankfully, because I was so rigid, I never really got out of control. That alcohol, aka, liquid courage, gave my peers a sense of confidence that I was lacking. Alcohol was a lot easier to get compared to pot, but I was determined and not willing to waiver. I was also still completely uncomfortable sexually since I was having serious body dysmorphia. The thought of exposing my body to anyone was unimaginable and therefore kept me innocent a lot longer than some of my peers.

I met several eligible prospects as soon as I started college. College was tabula rasa. My clean slate. There were many blind dates, one hit wonders and the one that got away, but I did, in the end, land the prince. The one that got away, in retrospect, would not have been as good a fit for me as my husband. I bring him up though because my fears and anorexia sabotaged any chance of this turning into a viable relationship. We were clearly enamored with each other, but our shyness prevented either one of us from taking it beyond friends.

Years later, when we discussed what could have been, we each acknowledged the missed opportunity. I firmly believe things happen for a reason, and I think I am right where I am supposed to be.

Regardless of how insecure I felt, I would not compromise, or settle when it came to what I wanted in a husband. My parents were married for sixty years. I grew up in a household of love, friendship, and laughter, and I knew that I would rather be alone than not find what they had.

This is not to say I was clear on how to identify who that would inevitably be.

BEING DEFLOWERED

After I started working, I began a long-distance relationship with one of my clients. This was definitely not encouraged but happened from time to time in the business of sales. Many conversions lead up to making a sale, and as a result, many working relationships turn personal organically. For whatever reason, this particular client and I hit it off from the beginning. He was located in another state, which immediately put me at ease and made the flirtation safe. We both had a passion for exercise and literature, which piqued my curiosity to no end. He talked about hiking and how scenic Chicago was. I too spent a lot of time hiking, so I appreciated our conversations.

Time went on, we had more and more dealings, and I was coming up with fire sales just to give me an excuse to call. He finally asked me, "what if I hop on a plane to New York, and we meet in person?" Suddenly there was a pit in my stomach. Of course, I was excited at the prospect of seeing him in person yet completely petrified as well, but I said sure thinking that there was no way this would come to fruition. But then it did.

This is like Match.com before it was a thing. As I was writing, I asked my husband what a good pen name for this guy would be for his role in my memoir. He blurted out Assman without a second thought, so Assman he is.

Assman told me that several people told him he looked like Jean Claude Van Damme. Immediately I surfed the web trying to imagine what he looked like and began to anticipate our meeting. This is a perfect example of why people are skeptical about online dating. People post pictures of themselves that are ten years old and compare themselves to much better versions of what they would want to look like. Assman was a case in point.

When I met him, I could see a slight resemblance if I were to leave my contact lenses out and stand a good twenty feet away. The comparison would be equivalent to me, comparing myself to Jennifer Aniston after I used Aveeno. I gave myself a pep talk and decided there is more to a person than looks, and although I thought I would be hanging out with a clone of Jean Claude, Assman is who I got.

We went to dinner at one of my favorite haunts. I remember the hostess innocently asking us where we would prefer to be seated. There was an isolated table upstairs, or a table situated next to other diners. I replied, "we will take the table upstairs, I know my shit is interesting, but I do not need people eavesdropping." Assman thought this answer was brilliant. He was clearly in love.

After dinner, I dropped him off at the hotel and arranged to pick him up in the morning so we could head upstate for a hike. Amazing how times change. Now I would never go hiking in the woods with a stranger, but this was the nineties. I do not remember the specifics, but it was a long drive, and I remember him asking me about my previous relationships which we had not discussed in depth. I revealed that I was a virgin while contemplating driving the car off the road. He could not believe it. He knew of my love for exercise, but now I had to tell him where my still being a virgin emanated from and about my eating disorder.

He reacted like he had won the lotto, and I felt like the Biggest Loser. I explained that I had been very self-conscious about my body. I had sabotaged every relationship that I had been in, so I did not have to show my body. He was very sensitive in his reaction and confided in me as well. He told me that he was divorced and had lost a child. His revelation made me feel less vulnerable since he was divulging private information about himself.

We got to our destination, a bed and breakfast upstate, and were shown to our room with one queen-sized bed. I knew I was going to be deflowered, and I was scared, but I was also relieved. I honestly wanted to get it over with, which I know is not the most romantic way to look at sex, but my organs were closing up, and I needed to get cracking. I remember going to a gynecologist appointment and the doctor telling me to relax. My response was, "nothing goes up there, nothing." This is going back twenty-five years, but what I can say is that I got a lot accomplished that weekend.

We hiked for about seven hours, because we got lost, and had to pay a random stranger on a bike in the woods for a map. Exhausted, we showered, and then I finally "did it." Yes, it hurt, and it was not so great for me, but he was patient, and I figured some shit out. I remember thinking, I wonder if I had an orgasm. If you ever have to ask that question, the answer is YOU DIDN'T.

I also recall, upon my return, my emotions were all over the place, and I was so grateful that he had to go back to Chicago.

He was smitten, and I felt smothered. This is why the long-distance relationship was the only way this could work for me. I was still figuring out my demons, and I needed to go slowly, which is unavoidable when there are eight hundred miles between you. One thing that was weighing on my mind and that I still regret is the way I handled the whole condom issue. After the first time, Assman refused or gave me a hard time about wearing a condom. He covered my eyes and said, "wearing a condom is like being blind." I was so worried that I would contract some sort of disease or get pregnant, but I could not get up the courage to insist he wear one. I felt careless, but I had no voice. I ended up getting tested, but this was the first indicator of how selfish he was. Later on, I would discover he had a temper, but because of the distance, it was not evident at first. Decades later, he confessed that he was a coke addict the entire time we were seeing each other. This was not detectable since we only saw each other twice a month, but his mood swings were obvious. He could cry at a poem and scream at me in the next breath. There were times he failed to pick me up on time at the airport, and as soon as I committed to him, he became less dependable. I did most of the traveling after the first six months.

This relationship went on for two years with many disappointments, but with my issues, this was the perfect introduction to adulthood. I loved being able to have a boyfriend but maintain my freedom too. It served my purpose at that time. I was finally getting to a point where I did not want to run from sex and my body, and I wanted to have someone around. Our relationship began to fall apart. I was so optimistic and naïve, and he was so damaged and pessimistic, the timing was just off. I do not regret any of it though.

Now I was ready to play the field and make up for lost time. There were other flings in between, but the next significant relationship was the one before I found my Prince Charming.

Let's call him Dickhead. Everyone has that one real heartbreak. This was mine. The name Dickhead is actually an oxymoron since, he had some erectile issues, which I will reveal in depth later. I am very bitter at the way this relationship ended and am calling him this because the way he broke up with me was just dickish.

Dickhead and I met in New York City, and we had a lot in common. We were both obsessed with nice things, working out, and food. We saw a ton of Broadway plays, ate all over the city, saw live bands, and truly had an exciting courtship. So here is what went wrong. Me still not comfortable in my own skin started a horrific habit of getting a new outfit before every time we saw each other. I also had my hair blown out before every time we got together. I was afraid if I was not dressed to the nines, or if I had a hair out of place, he would find someone better. He lived in Gramercy Park, and I took the train in on Wednesdays and then again on weekends. This relationship was costly in many ways. However, I was delusional and fell head over heels for something that was not even real. Most of it, I think was in my mind. Our feelings were not mutual, and Dickhead was careful to tell me every three months or so that maybe we should slow down. I would get sad for a minute and then just figure it would eventually turn my way.

I was finally in a good place with my eating until I started dating him. I totally relapsed and lost a good ten pounds over the course of our relationship. He became a trainer during our time together, and he was very focused on his diet. This caused me to fall back into bad, familiar rituals again. I started mirroring the way he ate, which was very clean, and once again found myself obsessing over my diet and restrictions. In addition, I felt inferior to Dickhead, so I was never relaxed. I remember this one time, I was staying over, and we had tickets to a play. Before the play, we had gotten intimate, so I wanted to shower before we went out. Thinking I was going in alone, I put on a granny shower cap so I would not mess up my blowout and guess who decides to join me? I was mortified. Definitely not the look I was going for, but I had to preserve the good hair.

On another occasion, I was wearing one of my three hundred dollar outfits—a Ralph Lauren leather houndstooth skirt with high heeled boots—and I had a wardrobe malfunction. I was all ready to hit the town until...wait for it...the slit in my skirt ripped on the train into the city. All the way up to the waist. I got off the train and proceeded to run through Penn Station like a lunatic, frantically looking for safety pins. Somehow, I managed to find some at a bodega. I asked a stranger to pin my skirt and tried to conceal my rip. I am sure I was walking funny, and I was miserable. Today if that happened my husband and I would be in hysterics, but at the time, I was so worried that I would not look good that I could not laugh at the hilarity of the scene. I do think I pulled it off undetected, but I will never know.

Next was the "rib incident." It is hard to believe that nothing perverted caused this, but during sex, I somehow ended up with a broken rib. I really do not know why it broke, but it did, and it freakin' hurt. Afterward, I could not breathe very well, had to wear a brace and go for physical therapy. After we broke up, the insurance company sent me a form to make sure my injury was not the result of a car accident. I would not be surprised if my reply is still circulating around the office. I wrote, there was no car accident, I broke my rib having sex with an asshole. I was distraught, and really did not think about what I was writing at the time, but I wish that was not documented in writing.

I think Dickhead broke it off with me because he knew I was way more serious than he was about our relationship. I think he also knew that his feelings would never be as strong as mine. He was engaged before dating me and was in therapy to figure out his relationship issues, which were causing his impotence. Timing is everything, and we were not in sync. Many times, he could not get it up. I am sharing this because even though there is no name attached, every single one of my friends will know this now, and that makes me happy. If you do not know who I am talking about, call me, I will make sure to reveal Dickhead's identity. Good thing I do not hold a grudge.

I have a good reason for being bitter. You see, when he broke up with me, he had stayed over for the weekend, we had sex, and then he told me it was over. Hence the nickname. How horrible is that? Did he need to get laid one last time? What was even worse is that I drove him to the train station after he dumped me. I was crying for the entire ride. He was consoling me, but why didn't I make him take a cab? He said I would only hear from him if his feelings had changed. One month later, he called. My heart skipped a beat, and we made plans to meet up. I assumed that he was missing me, and he had not realized how much he liked me until we spent some time apart.

Back to the salon, back to the mall for an outfit, he wanted me back. I headed into the city to have what I thought would be a wonderful night. We went to see a band, dinner, drinks, now it is 1 AM. I had no bag with me but rather a thong and a toothbrush. I say, "it's getting late should I head to Penn?" thinking I would be going back to his apartment. He proceeded to tell me nothing had changed so I better get to the train. Normally I do not lose it, but I said, "You told me you would not contact me unless things were different." They were not. I was heartbroken all over again.

I called one of my girlfriends, sobbing, not thinking I would ever be happy again. She was in New Jersey at a family function, but she left the event to come home and take care of me. I will never forget that gesture. She met me at my parent's house, and we did what girls do. We went to the diner to have a word-for-word recap, analyzing every double entendre to dissect what truly happened. After hours of discussion, there was only one next move. We needed psychic intervention. We paid a visit to Mercy, a psychic reader who would help me get my life back on track.

I wish the details were clearer, but I remember her eating a slice of pizza while she was detailing how I could remedy my love life. She told me to sleep with a pair of red panties and repeat a little chant. My friend who came along was going through a divorce at the time and was concerned her ex was going to kidnap her daughter. To safeguard her daughter, we had to go to the beach and throw a bottle with a note in it into the ocean. Yes, we both did our tasks.

I never spoke to Dickhead again, but her daughter was never kidnapped. This is okay because next came my Prince Charming, my husband, my soul mate.

MEETING MR. RIGHT

Now to get to the story you are dying to hear: How I met my Mr. Right (let's call my husband Superman).

After I dated Dickhead, I was very discouraged and down on love. Of course, I wanted to meet someone, but I just never thought I could feel such attraction and chemistry again. What I know now, is that when you find true love, it feels even better because it is reciprocated. However, we are not there yet, and I was not that open to more blind dates. My friend told me she was scrolling around on Match.com and saw a profile that sounded like a male version of me. Sort of sarcastic, but funny at the same time. Match.com was a minute old at the time, and I had no interest in putting myself out there. I was scared. I saw his profile, and I did think he was funny, but I was hesitant and told her, "not doing it." I offered up my email address though so we could correspond, but I did not have the courage to do more. She wrote him a note stating that her friend would be perfect for him, etc. He had joined for a one-week free trial because his friend was doing it and encouraged him to try as well. His reply was basically something to the effect of, "so you don't want to date me, but your friend does?" Somehow, we connected and started talking and have not stopped for sixteen years.

There are so many amazing things about my husband, but what stuck out from the onset is that he called when he said he would, yet he also gave me space. So anytime I got that scared feeling or did not know how I felt, days would go by, and I would inevitably miss him. He was reliable and did not keep me guessing. That guessing which I confused with excitement earlier was really disrespect and immaturity. There were no games with Superman, and after years of not being ready for the real thing, I was going to give love a chance. I fought the feelings to run when I got scared. This is when I realized that much of a relationship takes place in your own head. We decipher the meaning of another person's actions when more often than not, we are reading into things that are not there. After many conversations with men and women, I have learned that sometimes a guy does not call because he literally forgets or gets distracted. It honestly does not mean he changed his mind or likes you less. Women create scenarios based on watching too many movies on the Lifetime Channel. He is not necessarily having an affair, involved in a scandal, or living a double life. To this day, sometimes when my husband is going to be late coming home, he forgets to let me know so I can delay making dinner. He is consumed with what he is doing at work, and perhaps pulled into a meeting, but I sometimes get insecure and get resentful. I decide to go on strike, deciding not to cook. This lasts fifteen minutes until I get my shit together and realize that this is all in my head. I cook dinner, he walks in, and everything is fine.

I decided before we started dating, that I was no longer buying outfits, having my hair done and changing who I was so someone would like me. I wanted to feel like me and have someone love me for who I was. No one is to blame for my previous actions but me. That ritual stemmed from my insecurities. I needed to have more confidence and recognize that at some point (not as bad as the shower cap), but I was not always going to look perfectly coifed and sometimes I was going to wear sweats. This never seemed to be an issue with Superman, though. He was always complimentary and made me feel special.

He had his own insecurities and lacked confidence in different areas. We were very good for each other. His best friend happened to be a bit of a lady's man who had no trouble finding ladies but rather staying faithful to them. He advised Superman that it was very important to have good shoes, so they went shoe shopping, and he ended up with four hundred dollar Ferragamos to wear on our first date. This probably explains why Superman seemed to be sticking his foot in my face the whole time. Unfortunately, I did not notice the shoes, and he still talks about the blisters he endured to make a good impression.

We talked daily for hours on the phone and saw each other every weekend. Our relationship was consistent. I am a bit of a clothing snob, and as time went on, I gradually started redoing his wardrobe to all Ralph Lauren. This may sound superficial, and it sort of is, but he needed a woman's touch. His friends were very protective of him and made fun of his new rugby shirts and haircut, but he wanted to make me happy. I am hoping he thought he looked good too. Anyway, as we got to know each other, despite our different personalities, we had a lot of major stuff in common. I am very outgoing, and he is very reserved, but our values, loyalty, honesty, and hearts were the same. We are on the same intellectual level, although he will argue he is smarter. We have a similar sense of humor, and when we are not laughing together, we are usually laughing at some stupid thing I did.

What sealed the deal is that on the night he was supposed to meet my father for the first time, my father had a stroke and unfortunately passed away. Superman worked at a French bank, which of course I did not remember the name of, so I had the friend who set us up call every French bank in Manhattan. After many failed attempts, she finally found him. He took a week off from work and stayed by my side the entire time. He picked my brother up from the airport, and when I told Superman he could stay over, he felt it would be taking advantage of my vulnerability. Can you imagine? That really made me re-evaluate what I had been looking for and value what I had found. Ironically, his father passed away eight weeks later. I reciprocated, and our relationship took a turn. We had both endured a tragedy and helped each other through.

On our first date, I told Superman that I was writing a fitness book, and I asked him if he liked working out. He said yes, "I've been known to throw the weights around." Now I recognize what that means. This did not mean it was within the last decade or even two decades. If you ask him if he cooks, he will say, "yes, a few things," referring to the meatballs he made in fifth grade. He kept this charade going until he popped the question, and then he said about that fitness thing, "I was just kidding". He actually started working out again about two years ago though and is in better shape than I am, which is a little annoying, but he looks fantastic.

So along with the workout façade, he also mentioned that he liked to eat healthy. I must backtrack so that you will understand how this played out. My parents were married for sixty years. They went to Burger King every Friday for as long as I can remember. After my father passed, Superman asked my mother if he could take us out or do anything for us, and she said I would like to go to Burger King. So, we went, and I ordered a Whopper Junior and fries, and so does my mother. Superman ordered the now retired Veggie Burger, which still makes him gag when he talks about it, and fries. As we were talking and reminiscing, my mother said to him, "I would like to ask you a question." He replied, "ask me anything," so she asked him, "are you going to finish those fries?" Of course, he sacrificed them, but again once I officially became his girlfriend, the veggie burger was a thing of the past.

We really took our time getting to know each other, and contrary to all of my other relationships, the physical part was going very slowly. I could not tell if he was not attracted to me or just trying to be respectful. He claims that I jumped him, which I will deny, but at the three-month mark, I had to know if this was going to progress. He loves telling people that I attacked him, but I ask you, is it the three-date rule or the three-month rule? I just wanted to know where I stood.

We got into a rhythm, and at around the six-month mark, we were playing a game called questions, and my question was something like, "what would you want to say if you only had one chance to tell someone something that they didn't know?" I got up the courage to tell Superman that I loved him, and he handed me a card for our six-month anniversary, which had the same sentiments. In that very moment, I knew he was my prince.

At around the one-year mark, we had the discussion about moving in together. This was major for both of us. I was enjoying the time, and unbeknownst to me, Superman was planning to ask for my hand in marriage. I apparently foiled two previous attempts. I will tell you about the proposals, but when we decided to move in together, we had to get a bigger place. I was now in the market to sell my one-bedroom apartment.

We got a buyer almost immediately.

The man who bought my apartment had a very long commute to work, which was his excuse for buying a place to stay in during the week. He claimed that the commute was too much, but really it was where he was going to meet his mistress. I would never have known this fact if he did not have a heart attack on the bed that I sold to him. It happened his first night in my apartment (technically his at this point) with his not wife. He actually died. The only reason I learned about what happened is that I still had friends in the building. I am glad we heard because we had to get to the bank before they froze his assets. Superman and I ran to the bank to cash all of the checks he wrote and proceeded to move into our new two-bedroom.

Superman spent a long time picking out my ring without any advice. Back then, he used to listen to what I said. I must have shown him an antique ring that I liked, and he was able to find a one-of-a-kind ring that looked like an antique. If you ask him about it, he recites the facets and characteristics like he is reading off a script. He did a great job. I love the ring, but even more, our life and what it represents.

The first time he tried to propose, he had the ring in his pocket, and we were going out to the restaurant where we had our first date when a good friend called. She was having boyfriend issues, so me being me, I invited her along, and the ring stayed in his pocket. The next attempt was nearly a week later. He was in our apartment laying out little signs with arrows pointing to the bedroom saying will you marry me, and I was in between personal training clients, so I stopped in to change my workout clothes, and I ruined that one too. I did not even notice the signs (but I still have them).

They do say the third time is the charm...

When we finally moved into our apartment, it was Memorial Day weekend, and it was raining. We were putting things in order and grouting the tub. I had a moment of reflection, and I said to Superman, "isn't this perfect?" And he got down on one knee and said, "the only thing that would make it more perfect is if you would agree to be my wife." I did not know it was coming, and I was speechless and elated. I kept saying, "oh my God, oh my God." The poor guy was left wondering does that mean YES?

It did.

I mean, I thought we would get married, but I was not nagging, and he was getting the milk for free without buying the cow. I am so happy he wanted to buy the cow. We were officially engaged. At first, I mentioned not having a big wedding, perhaps doing a cocktail party. Then I went to a bridal showcase. Not much to say except at the end of the day, I had peacocks, smoke machines, and bagpipes. One could get carried away.

My parents had a really great marriage, and I hoped to have an equally happy marriage. I am not sure what I expected marriage to be like, but it has surpassed my expectations. My parents met each other when my mother was seven, and my father was eleven. My grandmother asked my dad if he would come and play with my uncle because my uncle was very shy. My father obliged, but when it made sense, he said I would rather play with your daughter than your son. I was amazed by their chemistry. They found the same humor funny, played Solitaire in the same room, liked the same goofy music, and just really enjoyed each other's company. I recall standing with my father watching my mother take in the neighbor's mail when they were on vacation. I asked him, "doesn't she ever get on your nerves?"

He replied, "that woman is a saint."

I did not understand their union then, but I do now. If anyone said anything negative about my husband, I would respond similarly. I really get it.

I knew they always loved being together, and that is what I wanted.

I sort of equate it to having a slumber party with your best friend every night. Do not get me wrong, sometimes the "pots and pans" as they call it of everyday life get monotonous, but I look forward to that key in the door every night. I still get excited to spend time with him, and I always choose him first.

After we got engaged, we went to another psychic. His name was Claude, and apparently, after he fell off a bicycle and cracked his head open, he was able to predict Princess Diana's death.

I put my engagement ring in my pocket so Claude would not have any idea that Superman and I were engaged. Soon as I sat down, he told me I could take the ring out of my pocket. Midway through Superman's reading, Claude stopped and gave him his money back. We had drawn pretty much the same cards, and we were destined to be together he said.

Do not roll your eyes back in your head. We have had our ups and downs like every couple, but this is the newlywed part of the tale, and I am telling it. There is a big learning curve when you move in together. You go from being on your own to living with someone else and their habits.

I will be the first to say, I can be annoying. I know you are not shocked by this revelation since my Type A personality has already been seeping out thus far. When anything breaks, gets chipped, gets a mark, etc. I want a new one, Federal Expressed if possible, and I will expect the shipping fee will be waived.

Superman is more of a go-with-the-flow type of a guy about those types of things. He has his own issues, let's be clear, but this is not one of them. Here is an example, I spilled some toxic cleaner on our counter in our first apartment, and the entire thing expanded and became deformed. He put a dish towel over it. I ordered a new granite countertop and sink.

The only saving grace is that I am gainfully employed and contribute to paying for my neurosis. He ends up having nice things, and I keep my sanity. A real win-win.

On another occasion, I was hanging up the laundry and noticed that my beloved's clothing rail was held together with duct tape. Of course, California Closets was at my house the next day.

Things like that can be frustrating on both ends. To Superman, these things do not matter, but as long as I fix things without involving him, all is fine. Living together requires compromise from both parties. The older you get, the harder it is to change your ways. Almost two decades later, I love living with Superman.

SLOW AND STEADY WINS THE RACE

At the ripe old age of forty-nine, I am doing a lot of reflecting. I am realizing that with each hard life experience, there is a lesson, and something is gained on the other side of the challenge. Too bad, you have to go through it without knowing the outcome in advance.

I remember how I was always wanting a boyfriend (in theory) and not having much success early in the dating arena. However, I was very determined to hold out for what I deemed important in a partner. Naturally, when I was fifteen, it was looks, but as time went on and dates were aplenty, behavior came into play. Those cool badasses became Dickhead and Assman, and I finally had the epiphany that Prince Charming did not have to treat me poorly to be cool. All those girls with serial boyfriends, who seemed to be so much more together early on, are now divorced or in unhappy marriages. That is a blanket statement and not true for many, but in my circle, when talking to many of my friends, they would not do it again with the same guy.

For centuries women's roles have changed from being subservient to equal-*ish*. I say "ish" because while we have an equal presence in the workforce now, in most instances, we are still the ones doing the food shopping, laundry, paying the bills, and handling childcare. So not really equal, but I have always thought men are the women God made wrong. They are the reject women. They cannot multitask successfully or handle much stress without losing their shit. So, they go in the reject pile and are called men. Although women can do it all,

I have found some of my friends ended up in horrible marriages. Verbally abusive, physically abusive, but stuck for financial reasons, or waiting until the kids are grown to get out.

I hated that it took me into my early thirties to find my guy, but I would definitely marry him again. I think by that stage, I understood what I wanted and what I knew would be important to create a lasting relationship. I wish I did not worry so much up until meeting Superman and enjoyed the process a bit more, but in the long run, it was worth holding out. When you take those vows, in sickness and in health, you do not really think of what that means because you are young and idealistic. In a marriage that lasts any significant amount of time, things will challenge your commitment. You better hope that you did not marry because of washboard abs alone.

I remember the moment I knew my husband was the one. It was on the night that I lost my father, and he showed up and stayed. Of course, having money makes life easier in many ways, but that should not be a factor why you marry someone. You want to be attracted to your mate, but when you love a person for their goodness, they become infinitely more attractive. You must have similar values. Especially if you plan on having children so you can form a united front (against the little monsters). After sixteen years with my husband, he is still my best friend, and I enjoy his company and look forward to being with him. I cannot imagine walking on eggshells around my husband or being unfaithful, or unhappy, or feeling trapped. Although we were happy, we were just starting out on our journey together when our moms started to show signs of wear and tear, and this made things hard.

PARENTING YOUR PARENTS

One of the hardest things in life happens when you have to start parenting your parents. Multiply that times two and you have my life.

Both my mother and my husband's mother had us after the age of forty. My mother was actually forty-eight when I was born. I am forty-nine now, and I am grateful that she went through with it, but I think she was nuts. I am so tired now, so I do not know how she handled an infant. I must add, she enjoyed every minute of it too. Not just because it was me, although I imagine that helped tremendously.

Watching your parent's health deteriorate is really difficult. My mother, who was highly intelligent, witty, well-read and educated, started to exhibit signs of dementia at age eighty. I was thirty-two at the time. At the end of her life, she did not recognize anyone, walk, eat on her own, or talk for at least three or four years until she passed at age ninety-five. My mother-in-law was in better mental health in the end, but she had heart issues, which lead to open heart surgery, and then Guillain Barre Syndrome, where she could not feel or use her extremities and that ultimately resulted in kidney issues. Combined, they would have made a healthy specimen, but as they were, they were a lot to handle.

It was not so bad at the beginning. His mom was not nearly as dependent as mine, and she was still living in her home. In fact, we made a weekly ritual of bringing my mother to either my mother-in-law's house or our house to play a heated game of Scrabble. Superman loves telling this story to anyone who will listen to illustrate just how competitive I am. As the story goes, we were playing our weekly Scrabble game. My mother was definitely losing her memory at this point, and she needed a lot of help with instructions. She also had misplaced her glasses. I had gotten up to make coffee, but I had already spotted my next move. While I was in the other room, Superman advised my mother on where she could use her tiles to score the most points. When I returned, she placed her tiles, under advisement from Superman, in the spot where I had planned to go next. I called him an asshole. My mistake was saying it loud enough that he heard. To this day, he still cannot believe that I did not apologize. I am really not sorry, though. I am of the opinion that each man is for himself in Scrabble and I had a Z I was going to put on a triple word score. He acts like he does not care about winning, but you should see how competitive he is when it comes to steps on the Fitbit. If I am ahead, he starts running in place until he passes me. Then he sends out a post on social media that he beat me.

Having both moms to look after made it twice as hard in one way. However, I think because we were both dealing with similar issues, there was also a sense of understanding and patience that might not have been present if there had been only one parent in need. If I was spending every weekend with my mother, I could understand if Superman got resentful that I was not around, and vice versa. Since he was in the same boat with his mother, this was never a problem.

There were times, however, that I got jealous of the way he would drop everything to take care of something for her that could have been handled by one of the staff members at her residence. She called him if the cable went out, or when she ran out of Polydent and things of that nature. I recall when I got a flat tire, and I called him he asked me, "don't you have roadside assistance?" I was pissed. I knew if it had been his mom, he would drop everything. In retrospect, I get it. I am very self-sufficient, and he has told me on many occasions this was one of the things that attracted him to me, but sometimes I wish I did not have to be so independent. How can I expect it to be both ways? A control freak with someone to lean on. Is that possible?

What became clear on both sides, is that our mothers fought our infant son for our attention. I recall one time I brought my son to my mother's place when he was a toddler. He wanted to play and run around, but she said she was bored and suggested things to do that he was too little to partake in. At this point, she did not really comprehend my relation to him and would have been quite pleased if I farmed him out to another family during our visit.

My mother-in-law was enamored with my son, so she would relish her alone time with him, but if she was not alone with him and the attention was detracted from her, she was jealous. She was also keenly aware and sharp and craved outside attention. We finally moved her, for her safety and our sanity, into an assisted living facility. She loved being at our house, and we hosted her for years every Saturday from early morning until after lunch. I had personal training clients during this time, so sometimes I would head to my mom's so she could have alone time with her grandson. This would ensure he was not calling for me, and he loved spending time with her.

I wish I had cherished that time more. It was fleeting. My mother's disease was progressing rapidly. On another Saturday, I took her out of the dementia unit for our weekly visit. I needed to go to Costco. Really any place we went that she was with one of her daughters was considered a field trip. Her entire life was very controlled, not unlike mine. That saying the apple does not fall far from the tree, is not lost on us. From my earliest memories, she had a checklist of things she needed to accomplish. She was so regimented that she even had a list to make sure she did not leave out one of the ten fruits she put in her daily fruit salad. She counted how many potato chips she ate and allowed my father to eat. They only had one square of chocolate at night, she measured everything. Not a shocker that I ended up with anorexia wouldn't you agree? Since the onset of her memory issues, she had forgotten she was neurotic, and she was now eating *everything* in sight. It was so weird to watch. In Costco, they give out a ton of free samples. Food is handed out in every aisle. With all of the free food, Jeannie (my mom) was in all of her glory until suddenly, she had an accident.

In the middle of Costco, she pooped herself. Of course, I was embarrassed, but more than that, I was paralyzed. Because she was unaware, within seconds, she had forgotten what had happened, and she was ready to find her next piece of free cheese. I abandoned my cart and somehow got her to the bathroom. She was a mess, and it was very hard to keep her still because she kept trying to leave the stall for more samples. I realized her clothing was ruined, but I could not leave her alone, so I quickly beckoned for a manager while simultaneously trying to hold the bathroom stall shut. I asked the manager to find some sweats, and some Depends while I kept her from escaping. I cannot really blame anyone for not wanting to help. I got the impression that the manager was regretting; he had not taken his break at that given moment. Begrudgingly, he delegated the chore to bring me some sweats, a top, socks, and shoes. The mess stunk, and it was disgusting. I was gagging from the smell and the mess. I threw her clothes out, changed her, and I was about to throw out her sneakers, which had shit all over them, when she said, "Hey, I want those." I lost it.

I screamed, "they are full of shit, and they are going in the garbage." She was mad until I handed her some more free cheese. I was truly shaken. This was the worst episode of her dementia yet. We managed to get out, but my nerves were shot. I got her home but decided that we would no longer leave the premises of her care facility on our visits. We could spend our time at her residence, so if there was another accident, I would have help readily available.

My mom was starting to make wandering outside of her facility a habit. She had her first fall with injuries when my son was about four making her around eighty-five. She broke her wrist as a result. I was on a playdate when it happened, and not close to home, but Superman saved the day. He stayed with her at the hospital. He made it a point of telling the administrators that she had dementia because she was very agitated most of the time. She did not understand where she was, so she kept getting off of the gurney to walk around. She also made poor Superman answer the same question more than a dozen times. This was worse than Kryptonite. They waited two hours before the X-ray technician emerged from the X-ray room. I still wonder if he was taking a nap because there did not seem to be any patients before my mother, so it was very odd. Anyhow he brought her into the room with the X-ray machine and told her to remain very still while he went into an adjacent room to take the scans. I think he felt like he was being punked because she could not remember to stay still. She kept moving her hands, and it took every bit of restraint for the technician not to break her other wrist. Her actions were perfect retribution for making her wait so long.

At one point, my mother started spending time with a man who was also a resident in the facility. She mistook him for my father, but obviously, he was not. The caretakers eventually told us that my mother and the man slept together, which I found incredibly disturbing. He did not have any issues with memory loss, so if you ask me, he was just a dirty old man. I was appalled because I thought he was taking advantage of my mother. Frantic, I called my sister and told her we have to do something. Then we both took a step back from the situation. We had to admit our mother looked happy and I thought to myself, she is not going to get pregnant, and if she thinks she is reunited with my dad, is there any harm being done? I was not sure, but as it turns out, her ninety-one-year-old boyfriend got moved to another facility. I was worried this would upset her, but thankfully she did not remember.

The next time she fell, we were not as lucky. I had threatened the facility on numerous occasions that if they did not get her an anklet with an alarm on it, they were going to be sued. I am not litigious, but she had broken out over twenty times at this point. Their plastic sign, on the unlocked door, that said STOP was not cutting it. Her residence was located right next to the expressway, so she was in real danger every time she got loose. They finally complied, and she put the ankle bracelet to the test.

Even with the alarm on, it took them forty-five minutes to get to her. It was two AM, and you know that a phone call, when you are not single, at that hour is never good news. I picked up the phone, and they proceed to tell me that my mother had fallen and hurt her knee. I popped up, got dressed, and headed over to the hospital. When I got there, I found she had a bloody head, a broken nose, four missing teeth, and the bone in her knee was completely exposed. I am glad she was not aware of what happened. I burst into tears and found the doctor who put twelve stitches in her knee, eight on her lip and set her nose. I called my brother in Seattle, not knowing if she would pull through. As I was sitting there looking at her, she looked up at me innocently and said, "I am not having fun here, would you like to go somewhere else?"

I laughed and cried. This was my mom. A pleasant, warm person who just emanated goodness. I stayed until seven thirty AM, and then felt it was finally a respectable time to call my sister, who was also local, and tell her what went down. The only reason I did not wake her in the middle of the night was because I knew, as the children living nearby, we would have many sleepless nights ahead of us. We would have to divide and conquer. She came right over to relieve me and take the next shift. MRI's and X-rays were next, and my mom had to drink that awful contrast. The contrast fluid you have to drink for the test is nasty, but from sip to sip she could not remember, so my sister kept saying, "Mom you must be thirsty. Have a drink." Skillfully done I might add. She managed to get sixty-four ounces of that horrible liquid down her, so the doctors could make sure she had no internal injuries.

Despite looking like she had been jumped by a gang, she was released after a few days in the hospital and moved to the same facility my mother-in-law was in, while we waited to have her transferred to a nursing home. My mother was plagued with a series of UTI's and bedsores in the interim because the facility (my MIL's assisted living place) was not equipped for that level of necessary care. However, there was no way I could send her back to the residence where the fall occurred. Finally, three months later, after frequent infections and difficult visits, she moved into her last home, a nursing home where her quality of life went way down. She never walked again, and her memory took a dramatic decline. Soon she would not be able to recognize us, but she lived an additional seven or eight years.

Just as our fathers died within eight weeks of each other, our mothers died within a little over a year apart. My mother-in-law had her wits about her until the end. Right before Superman and I got engaged, she had to have open heart surgery. I remember the timing so well because when we went to show her my engagement ring, she was recuperating from the heart surgery. She was staying with my now estranged brother-in-law who had just gotten out of jail for beating his wife. He was a prize. I am happy to say he was adopted, so we do not share his genetics. If you ever questioned nature versus nurture, my husband and his brother are proof that genetics (nature) plays the bigger role. They could not be more opposite. My husband abides by the rules, is honest, polite, considerate, and has a mild temper. My estranged brother-in-law, was explosive, violent, took drugs, was truant, and at the end of the day, was negligent and stole from his mother. Let's call him Satan. We had to have him evicted from her house, because he wanted the house, and was not addressing her medical needs. His biggest concern was how he could get the deed to her house.

She made a great recovery from the open-heart surgery. The next illness that plagued her was called Guillain Barre Syndrome. She was unable to feel her extremities, and she lost the use of her arms and legs for a good two months. We feared that because Satan did not get her to the hospital immediately, but rather gave her a bucket to urinate in, that the effects may have been worse than if she had been treated immediately. However, as soon as my husband learned of her symptoms, she was taken to the hospital, diagnosed, and in rehab within a day. She bounced back from that as well, but she remained very unstable on her feet. We were nervous transporting her around and getting her in and out of the car. Regardless, she was at my house every Saturday from the moment my son was born until the last year of her life. She was the grandmother you always hear about. She spoiled my son, of course with things, but even more so with attention. No matter when I walked in, they were either playing a board game, watching SpongeBox (as she liked to call SpongeBob), playing baseball in the house (unbeknownst to me until later), etc. Truly just playing together, which is every kid's dream.

She was a lot different as a grandmother than she was as a mother. I think she was remorseful about how she treated my husband while he was a kid. To deflect some of the negative attention that Satan was attracting, she felt like she had to throw Superman under the bus to dissipate the punishment. If my father-in-law was yelling at Satan, my mother-in-law would point to Superman, and say well this guy's no angel either. Superman would look at her perplexed and say, "what did I do?" She said she regrets it. Superman forgave her quicker than I did. I never showed my displeasure, and I loved her with all of my heart, but it hurt me to know she was tough on him. He was a great son until the very end. Watching him care for her assured me that we would have an enduring marriage. He actually took her to have her toenails clipped monthly. She had a similar incident to my mother's Costco fiasco, at my house. Thankfully I was not there, but let's just say Superman and I had enough shit to last a lifetime.

She was funny without trying to be. The first time I met her, she answered the door without her dentures in, gnawing on an ear of corn. I think I loved her from that second on. She was overweight for most of the time I knew her, and she loved telling other people that they were fat. This never bothered me until she told me it looked like I put on a few, and then all bets were off. It took me a good six months to let that go, and still, when I think about it, it makes me mad. She never understood my eating issues, and really who would, they are weird, but it hurt me all the same. She told the podiatrist that he got fat, and in the waiting room, she poked my husband and using her regular voice said, "look, Big Mama is in the house." I think he wanted to disappear. When my mother said things like that, I mouthed that she was crazy and got away as quickly as possible. It was truly so embarrassing, but I am sure at some point I will be doing that too.

Satan ended up stealing half of her life savings. After that happened, we stopped all communication with him and have not spoken to him in sixteen years. She was in her right mind when she expressed that she did not want him to be notified when she passed. It was such a shame, but a relief that we no longer had to engage with him.

I recall a time when both moms were somewhat stable, I was newly pregnant, and I had decided it would be so nice to share in the excitement together. I picked up both mothers and brought them to the mall to help me get my layette. Truth be told, I did not even know what a layette was, but I thought this would be something we could all do as a family. We headed over to the mall, and as soon as they got out of the car, I realized I might have made a bad call. My mother started sprinting to the mall, and my MIL had to stop every few feet to catch her breath. When we got inside, my mom took off in one direction, while my MIL found a seat on one of the benches in the mall and started eating a banana that she conveniently had in her purse. I wish this were an exaggeration.

We finally got upstairs to the infant area, and I explained to the sales clerk that I was here to prepare my layette. My mother immediately said, "why don't we wait until the baby comes out to see what it needs." Conversely, my MIL said, "we should get multiple sizes in every color of everything." She does not really take no for an answer, so we did. Afterward, I called my husband and told him his mother was out of control. We spent enough money to get a free bassinet from Saks Fifth Avenue. He assured me we would mitigate the damage the following day. I brought home contraptions that I had no idea what they were for. A wipe warmer? Really? I will never forget that day, it was very comical.

We had many joyful years with my mother-in-law, and she actually seemed really happy. We sold her house, and she moved into an assisted living facility. She really embraced the environment and got very involved with the community. She went on every field trip, ran movie night, called bingo, and made a happy life for herself. She was very outspoken and tended to rub some people the wrong way. She was also able to instill guilt if we did not visit as frequently as she liked. This was not because we did not want to visit, but we both worked full time and had a toddler. Regardless, she was not shy if she felt neglected. We did make it there every week, mostly multiple times a week, and all of it was good. When her kidneys started to fail is when things took a turn. She definitely went into a depression, and I cannot say I blame her. She had a year of UTI's, bedsores, and really difficult times, however, I can still see her smiling face when we walked down the hall to visit. I really felt like she was my mother too, and I miss her a lot.

Although Superman and I were now orphans, and we were really sad, there was some relief in not having to care for both of our moms. I do feel guilty about writing that, but it is true. Taking care of them took up the majority of our weekends, for close to fourteen years, and that is a lot of pressure on a marriage. Now it is time to talk about the other half of our weekend... taking care of our son.

FIRST COMES LOVE, THEN COMES MARRIAGE, THEN COMES...

While we were caring for the "wonder twins," we had our son. Many people warned me about having children at my elevated age of thirty-five, and we were concerned that I might have trouble conceiving. They were very wrong. I got married on September third, and we decided to start trying November tenth. I got pregnant on November tenth. Not that I was not excited, but I really wanted to be a newlywed for a little while. Thinking it would take a year, my emotions were all over the place about suddenly being pregnant. You know my husband thought he was a total stud and walked around pretty much saying, "first try. I knocked her up on the first try." After he stopped focusing on his virility, however, reality set in and he was in a panic too.

I had one of the worst pregnancies ever. I was sick from the beginning. My first symptom was nausea, which I thought was supposed to happen only in the morning. What moron came up with the name morning sickness? Let me guess. A man, perhaps? Everything that contained milk tasted sour to me. So pretty much there went my entire diet. No more cereal, coffee, frozen yogurt. Then I started taking the prenatal vitamins, which left a metallic taste in my mouth. Carbs were the only thing that did not bother me. There was a brief period when I was meeting a good friend of mine weekly at the diner because grilled cheese and French fries were one of the only meals I could keep down. I actually stopped calling my friend and started bringing a book because I wanted to eat the entire platter of fries myself.

One night Superman and I will never forget, is the night we had a couple over who were newly dating. They were making out in my driveway for twenty minutes before they came inside. Feeling like a whale and wanting to be kissed too, I asked Superman if he tasted the metal when he kissed me. He said he did. I wish he had lied. The couple came in and, knowing I tasted like metal, I cried the entire evening while we watched a movie.

The next catastrophe was in my seventh month. I was still training several clients. During a session, I excused myself and threw up numerous times. My client happened to be a doctor, and it turns out that I had food poisoning. I started having premature contractions, and I had to go to the hospital to have IV liquids administered to counter the dehydration and stop the contractions. I am going to add a little girl drama. This food poisoning happened right before my baby shower, which was supposed to be a surprise. They had to tell me about the shower, so the surprise did not send me into labor with the extra stress. Perfect time for a friend of mine to call me up and scream at me for allowing another friend to throw my SURPRISE baby shower. The key term here is *surprise*. I had nothing to do with who threw the shower, but she told me she could not forgive me, and we have not been friends since. Despite the drama, I thoroughly enjoyed my shower. I had to finish out my pregnancy from hell at home. I was petrified to become a mom, but I was at the point that I needed my son to get the hell out. There was no longer room for the both of us.

Superman had started a new job since I had needed him a lot during this time, and his two-hour commute was getting old. This was tough because I went from being really independent to feeling very needy. Thankfully he landed something a mere fifteen minutes away. I was thrilled, but I am not so sure he was. His new company was very understanding. They kept trying to throw him a baby shower, but between all of my complications, I think they scheduled and rescheduled a shower three times until they finally pulled it off.

I started having contractions ten days before my due date, and my doctor sent me to walk the mall for hours and hours. I was not dilating at all, and I was miserable. They admitted me and gave me Demerol. I finally had a brief respite from my pain. I was high as a kite and could not stop laughing. Superman was lying on two folding chairs covered in a tiny blanket, and I keep looking over at him and repeating, "I have to focus," and then I would burst out laughing. He sounds a little bitter when I remind him of that part of the story, but I was the one delivering his son, so I do not feel too bad. The next morning, I still had not progressed, and they gave me Pitocin. Finally, it was time to push. I was in excruciating pain even with an epidural and guess who is not moving. My son came out stubborn and has not really changed. Before giving birth, his blood oxygen level began dropping, and it was quickly determined that I had to have an emergency C-section.

After twenty-six hours of labor, my boy was born. He was six pounds eight ounces, a ten on the Apgar, but he had to go into the NICU since he had not exited through the birth canal, and his breathing was labored. That was really emotionally hard. I was desperate to hold him, but I would have to wait. Many hormones are floating around during pregnancy, and the separation made me cry. Everything made me cry.

They put me in a room with another mom who had her baby beside her, and I was hysterical. The nurse actually yelled at me for crying, but I wanted to be with my baby. Eventually, we were reunited, and I remember staring at him in awe. Every feature was perfect. A little miracle.

The lactation consultant came in and tried to show me how to work the breast pump, but I had it on for one minute and decided that there is a good reason formula was created. I felt like a cow with those pumps attached to my boobs. I remember looking down at my son and thinking he was the most beautiful baby I had ever seen. It is amazing that everything came out so perfectly. I know why God made him so cute. It is because he was colicky. His adorable face was his life insurance policy, so we did not kill him.

Superman and I had no clue whatsoever how to take care of an infant. My mother had Alzheimer's, so she was not there to help, and my eighty-something year old mother-in-law had limited mobility, so we had to hire a baby nurse.

We are going to refer to her as Maleficent. She was not horrible, but she sort-of blackmailed us once she realized that we had no clue what we were doing. She was from Trinidad, with a heavy accent. We both had a hard time understanding her. She loved telling us how perfect her last charge had been. She made it clear that her previous ward was not colicky and caring for our baby was asking a lot from her. Superman and I still remember her chanting while rubbing our son's armpits something about him having the gripes. We did not know what the hell she was talking about, but FYI gripes is another name for gas. Every time I am in CVS I cringe when I see gripe water.

Baby nurses are very pricey. I think it was a thousand dollars a week, but we were desperate. Not to mention my C-section hurt, and I was exhausted. I was overwhelmed, to say the least. I was trying to get into some sort of routine. The baby started crying one night, and for the first time since we were home, I did not pop up like I had been doing previously. I was lethargic, but I got the baby and handed him to Maleficent. She noticed that the blanket he was swaddled in was very warm. She asked me if I had just taken it out of the dryer. Apparently, I was burning up. I had a 102.7 fever, so I was headed back to the hospital. I had seven blankets on me, but I was still freezing, and my teeth were chattering. I woke up in a pool of sweat. My incision was infected. Now Maleficent was Snow White because we were in trouble. We begged her to extend her stay, which she did begrudgingly. However, we were pretty much kissing her ass so that she would not leave. While in the hospital, I was pumped with tons of IV antibiotics to get rid of the infection.

Finally, I went home and started to recover, but for once, I had no appetite. I would take a bite of food and have to go to the bathroom immediately. I lost forty-two pounds in three weeks. I went to the gynecologist and a gastroenterologist, and they diagnosed me with post-partum depression. I was depressed, but not over the baby, rather over feeling sick. I was not able to keep food down, so I was totally exhausted and depleted. After a month, they finally figured out that I had contracted C-Diff. Clostridium Difficile Colitis, caused by an overdose of IV antibiotics, or germs from the hospital. It wiped out all of my good bacteria and caused constant diarrhea, nausea, fever, and abdominal pain. This would take over a year to get it out of my system. I called my sister in desperation. She came over immediately, and she told me after I was out of the woods, that she was really scared. She looked into my eyes and genuinely did not know if I would recover. I started the prescribed protocol, and I was beginning to feel better, but as soon as I stopped taking the medicine, it came back with a vengeance. My sister reached out to my psychiatrist who had treated me for my eating disorder a decade ago. She told him she was afraid I was suicidal, and he said, he would like to help, but he did not have room in his schedule. I would love to publish his name. Thank God for the internet because we contacted the Post-Partum Resource Center of Long Island, and they sent over the first of several doulas. Maleficent was too expensive, and we could not keep her. The doulas not only became my friends, but they were amazing with my son, they taught me how to care for him and allowed me to rest so I could recover. There were two in particular that alternated days, so I had someone with me every day for the first three months of my son's life.

Once a private person, I now had strangers in and out of my house. My brother and his wife, who were scheduled to go to Japan for work, dropped everything to come all the way from Seattle to help. I will never forget what my family did for me.

I was seeing a top doctor, according to *New York Magazine*, who continued to increase my antibiotics so that I was now dependent upon them. By the end of this dreadful story, I was taking twelve pills a day. I pulled Superman aside one night, thinking I might not make it through, and told him he could re-marry.

He asked, "how soon?"

I tried to make light of it, but it was no joke. I was now talking to therapists, psychiatrists, gynecologists, gastroenterologists, but I was not getting better.

That fire that you have witnessed throughout my tales was almost out. By chance, I found out there was going to be a lecture at the hospital where I had given birth by an expert in treating C-Diff, so in a last attempt, I made a fake badge and snuck in. I was surrounded by doctors. I had a mini tape recorder and got the entire talk on tape. The doctor who was presenting (I think he was from New Hampshire) had actually figured out a cure for my sickness. When he finished, I approached him, and after explaining my struggles, begged him to take me on as a patient. He felt sorry for me but was unable to help due to logistics and limited funding. At least now I had the formula. I just needed the doctor who would be able to get me on the protocol and prescribe the proper medication.

My doctor was too arrogant to listen to what I had learned. From thirteen to nineteen, I babysat for a women who I remembered had a vast network of resources. I practically raised her kids. She was like a second mother to me and very invested in helping me get better. Her brother-in-law was a doctor in Manhattan, and she got a recommendation from him. Thankfully, she offered to drive me into the city and wait with me on multiple occasions. I was so weak that I would not have been able to get myself to his office, and Superman had already missed so much work at his new company. He turned out to be the right doctor. The doctor who understood the disease and helped me to get my health back on track. After a full year, I finally was out of the woods.

This experience scarred me. I had flashbacks of my hospital stays, my teeth chattering incessantly, and the constant chills that I suffered for twelve months. I was better physically, but I had a lot of depression to work through. I was depressed over missing the first year of my son's life while I was struggling to get better and could not enjoy what was supposed to be a magical time.

Truth be told, I may have had challenges even if I had been healthy. Adjusting from being self- centered and only worrying about yourself to caring for a helpless infant is daunting for most. However, couple that with a severe illness, I imagine it would have thrown anyone into a tailspin.

I told Superman that I did not want to have any more children. I could barely believe that I had recovered. He ran to get a vasectomy because my being sick was no picnic for him either. I could not believe he did not want to leave me. You take the vows in sickness and in health, but I had put them to the test, and he was there unequivocally. I felt so guilty for causing so many problems. The circumstances were beyond my control, but what a way to begin our first year of marriage and parenthood.

During this time, I felt so lost. The familiar routines that had been my life for thirty-five years were out the window. I think the only reason I did not reprimand myself for not exercising like I had been doing obsessively since I was fourteen, was because I was so thin from not being able to eat, that I gave myself a pass. At least until I got some of my strength back. All those years of focusing on myself shifted to focusing on my son and finding a new normal. This was not an easy feat, but I finally decided to ask for help. They say it takes a village and I no longer wanted to be a martyr.

THE ALIEN HAS LANDED

Now that I was finally feeling better, I could focus my attention on my baby, who was absolutely perfect in every way. It really is something to create a human being. He is a blessing, and it made my family feel complete. I had to figure out how to meet his needs, maintain my marriage, and not lose my identity. For someone used to working on a schedule, having a baby is a huge eye-opener. You are no longer in charge. You are at your child's beck and call twenty-four-seven (thirteen years later, still the case). Becoming a mom was hard for me because I did not know how to incorporate my needs with the baby's needs. I still wanted to socialize, I still needed to exercise, I had to work, yet I had this dependent little guy that I brought into the world. He had to take priority.

What I learned from my sickness and continue to acknowledge is that I could not do everything myself. Although it is hard to ask for help, if I was going to strive and thrive, I had to say yes when people offered to help. I also wanted to make sure that I was able to have alone time with Superman. It is sort of ridiculous that I worried because newborns sleep a lot. However, we went from dating to husband and wife, having a kid, and buying a house within a year, so we were still newlyweds and wanted to have time together.

We found a babysitter when my son was about six months old and started to have some date nights again. I still had the C-Diff, but my symptoms were under control as long as I was on the medicine. I returned to work after the standard three-month maternity leave. Things were falling into place. Thankfully, I had a daycare facility at my job. I got to be around adults for most of the day, but I was still able to feed my son lunch and know that he was a floor away if I needed a hug. Although I was not a natural at parenting, I adored him. I may not have known how to work the diaper genie and the wipe warmer, but my love was instinctual, and I was finally feeling that I was moving in the right direction. Looming in the recesses of my mind, however, was the constant fear of my disease getting worse. The fact that I still had the infection caused me tremendous anxiety. Although contained, it was still overtaking my body. I was very concerned that I would never be able to get off of the medication, or that my body would become resistant to the antibiotic from overuse. When I was not consumed with worry about my health, my attention was spent on my son.

My weekends, which used to be all about me were now trips to the local animal farm and the Children's Museum. To take care of both of our needs, I made plans every weekend with a different mom and kid. I was actually shocked when I would call to make plans, and a mom would say I cannot go out today, "we are having a family day." Please do not misunderstand, I could not love my family more, but I was so used to socializing and being out and about, I could not imagine just staying home. What did they do all day?

On the days that I spent watching my son at McDonalds's in the play area, Superman got to do his own thing. I was a little jealous but thankful I had mommy friends to compare notes. I felt like I was a good mom, yet still getting to hang out with a friend. As time went on, some of the plans happened at my house or the house of another mom with their kid. When the children were not mobile, this was totally perfect, but when they started to ambulate, I uncovered another level to my stress. The funny peculiar, not funny ha-ha, thing is I was not worried about the safety of the kids or being able to entertain. I was concerned that the child would get crayon on my wall or throw a video game controller at my TV, missing it by a millimeter. That actually happened, so do not judge. I wanted to put the kids in a cage. Of course, I swallowed my anxiety and let them be kids, because I am more rational than I am crazy, but this was not easy. The older they got, the bigger and greater the damage became, baseballs through windows, gutters clogged by baseballs, etc. Then something happened that put everything in perspective.

IN SICKNESS AND IN HEALTH

All of those afternoons that I was out with my son, Superman had nothing to do to occupy his time. He did not have hobbies to keep him busy, so after stressful visits with his ailing mom, he would go to a bar to unwind, have a drink, talk to the bartender and play Quick Draw. He would also run errands and take care of things that he did not accomplish during the work week. He really was not seeing his childhood friends because they all had families too, so they had started going in different directions. His best friend was a girl that it turned out had feelings for him, and unbeknownst to me apparently blamed me for ruining their friendship and was not a fan of mine. I learned that one night when they went out for a few drinks to catch up, and she made a pass at him. Although I completely trusted him, the dynamics of their relationship did a one-eighty, and she did not understand that being a husband and father was a completely different role. He could no longer be her stand-in date or drinking buddy. Hence the resentment she was harboring towards me. I do understand that if you are not a parent, you cannot really imagine how your life shifts. You think you can pawn off the kid on someone else, so you can go out and do what you always did. Clearly, this is not the case, and at least in our experience, we did not want to have someone else watching our child. We both wanted to be home as a family.

As my son was getting older, so were our moms. Our life was getting more complicated, and they required a lot of attention. There was no downtime from stress. Transporting my mother-in-law was not an easy task. She had difficulty getting in and out of the car and was not that mobile. In addition, my mother was still in the nursing home and had to be visited weekly. All of this stress was boiling inside of Superman. Women confide in other women and talk things out until they feel relieved. Men swallow their feelings. I was there to listen, but he was not talking. He never wanted to burden me, and he did not always understand that I wanted to help, listen, and be there for him. I understand now that I cannot necessarily fix everything, and sometimes he just needed to be heard. I knew that he was preoccupied and had a lot on his mind, but I did not know the extent. While Superman thought he was protecting me, he was shutting me out which was equally, if not more, difficult to handle.

Well into our marriage, over the ten-year mark, Superman started to have some mysterious health issues. He was throwing up, sleepy but had insomnia, and just did not feel like himself. We went for test after test, and his blood tests were erratic. I thought this was a direct result of all of the stress. There were days when he was totally fine, and then others where he was out of it, and not right. I spent hours and hours trying to diagnose him and determined that he had fermented gut syndrome. Do yourself a favor and do not go on the internet with your symptoms. I promise you no good will come out of trying to diagnose stuff yourself. I cried and cried, thinking he had cancer, or something worse. Determined to get to the bottom of this, I got him into a specialist in Ohio. He had forty-five vials of blood drawn. I am not exaggerating. He was told he was in adrenal fatigue and had mercury poisoning. He came home with supplements and instructions on how to get his health back. We were also instructed to immediately go to the hospital if he became symptomatic. There is no need to go into detail, so I am going to skip ahead to when the shit hit the fan.

It was a day in January, which was a floating holiday. School was closed, I was off, and thought he was working. He seemed off when I got home and at eight-forty-five PM, fifteen minutes before the Urgent Care closed, I insisted we run over there. They promised to wait for us. My son (who was about ten at the time) was not too happy being dragged out in his pajamas, but I wanted the doctor to see what Superman was experiencing while it was happening. I always considered myself intuitive, but when the doctor asked Superman if he had been drinking and I said no, Superman said yes, my whole world went BLACK. I honestly did not know what to do. I burst into tears but quickly wiped them away because my son was watching and listening to everything. Regardless of how badly I wanted to roll up in a ball and not deal with what was in front of me, I had to put on a façade, so my son did not get scared. I was angry and embarrassed that I did not pick up on his drinking. How could I be so stupid?

How the hell did I not figure this out? A wave of panic overtook me. The solid foundation that my marriage was built on had a crack. I left something out earlier that I am now going to admit. Back when I had my tarot card reading with Claude, we were allowed to ask one question on a piece of paper that he would address at the end of the reading. My question, even back then, was if Superman's drinking would interfere in our marriage. The reason I had worried about this was that his friends were partiers, and I was afraid he was going to miss that lifestyle. Claude did not think I needed to worry. Maybe I did not figure it out because I did not want to see the drinking? The reason I am willing to discuss this is because this is life people. I did not want to tell my story and leave a significant part out because I am not ashamed. Unfortunately, this is how we learn.

Some of us are overeaters, anorectics, alcoholics, drug abusers, abused by a spouse, abusing a spouse, have kids with issues, have kids on drugs, have homosexual kids, have financial hardship, are estranged from family members, are having affairs or are being cheated on by a partner. No one who lives remains unscathed. There was one thing I always felt in my heart with Superman, and that was trust. I never questioned it, and now I found myself trying to figure out how I missed all of the signs. I was hurt beyond belief because there were times where I questioned if he had been drinking, and he looked me in the eye and said no. I felt betrayed. HOWEVER, when I was in the midst of my eating disorder, I lied, hid my eating, avoided and deceived, so I understood why he did it. He was also remorseful and ashamed, and I still loved him. In that moment, I could not fathom a life without Superman. He is my life. I mean, could I go on? I am sure I could, but I did not want to without him. For once I did not have the answer, and it shook me.

I decided that we could conquer this if we both agreed to try. He committed to working things out together and did not want to lose what we had either. The trust took a long time to come back because I was afraid that if I left the house or did anything where I was not watching, he would sneak off. He made a very valid point one day. He said if I want to drink, I will find a way, so you are going to have to let go and let God and trust that I will do the right thing. This experience, although harder than anything, did wonders for my marriage. I realized what is important and how quickly the rug can be pulled out from under you. We are so much stronger and honest with each other today. I felt such enormous fear over losing my marriage that now I do not take any day for granted. Ever.

As I debated back and forth about including this part, I felt I had to, to be truly transparent. I questioned whether it was my story to share since it happened to him, but it drastically affected me. I asked Superman for permission. He was hesitant at first until I said you should be so proud, not embarrassed. I am so proud of him, and this experience taught us how strong our marriage is and how much we wanted to be together. Not only did we have to figure out how to regain our footing, but we had to re-visit our social life.

Without wanting to broadcast that we were no longer drinking, we had to make decisions about who it might be difficult to hang out with and who would be non-pressuring. I do not think it is ever intentional, but people tend to push alcohol to justify their own consumption. I have always felt this, because again, with my eating disorder, every drink was one hundred calories to me, which I would always rather eat than drink. It was one thing when people said to me every party has a pooper, but I did not want Superman to feel uncomfortable. I made a choice that I would be willing to stop socializing with anyone who made him feel uncomfortable. Although he said it would be fine if I wanted to drink, as a commitment to our solidarity, I will not drink in his presence.

A SEASON, A REASON, A LIFETIME

At first, after we stopped drinking, we spent a lot of weekends at home, or together as a family. I honestly did not want Superman to be in a vulnerable setting until he felt he had a better handle on things. After a certain amount of time elapsed, we had to figure out how to get back in the game so that it was comfortable for both of us. There are certain people who come into your life for a specific purpose, others for a certain time frame like high school or college, and then there are the lifers.

I have been blessed in my life to still have friends who I have known since I was a toddler. Although we have gone in different directions, we have managed to stay in touch in a nostalgic and poignant way. When we get together, it is as if no time has passed. Those are your lifers. The people you cannot imagine not being involved in some aspect of your life. Lifers have somehow impacted your life and contributed to who you are as a person.

Then there are other friends you meet along your journey when you are pursuing a specific interest who share your passion, and for that time you have a lot in common. For me, when I was dieting, I spent a lot of time with chronic dieters and exercisers who were equally engaged and did not get bored while I incessantly talked about my weight and struggles. They were equally obsessed. Conversely, when I was trying to recover from anorexia, because of my competitive nature, some of those friendships became toxic for my recovery. I had to be around people who did not focus on food and losing weight. They were a season. This was the same scenario we were faced with but around alcohol rather than food. It was hard to be around a group of friends who were drinking bottles of wine while we drank soda.

A few things had to happen for us to find our way. As a couple, we discussed if an outing would prove to be fun or stressful, and we evaluated our plans as they came up. When you are in a season, you may not recognize that the friendship may not be as enduring as originally perceived. I could not foresee that some of my friends who partied too hard would prove to be challenging for Superman to be around. There was no question. I made my decision that they could work with us or we could agree to go our separate ways. Usually, people are mostly consumed with themselves and what you perceive to be a huge deal is really minute in the scheme of things. The majority of our friends could care less about what we were drinking, but just wanted our company and vice versa. A non-issue. Most of the dilemma resides in your own head, caused by your own judgements.

This really resonates for every phase of life. When I went to work, my co-workers and I started spending time together. When I was single, I spent more time with my single friends since we had a common interest in meeting new potential love prospects. When I became a mom, I made other mommy friends. When I felt depressed after I had my son, I spent time with other moms in similar boats, who normalized my feelings and helped me get through that tough period. I lost touch with them, but they were a season.

Superman does not ask me to stay home all the time, but he asks that I do not necessarily drag him along. This was an adjustment for me since I always like to be with him. At first, I felt weird showing up to parties without him. However, when I stopped worrying about what other people thought and started making sure that our own needs were met, this ended up being the key to our success. I always had him to watch my son, I did not have to worry about him being bored, I could circulate freely, and he was in his comfortable place, our home. And really almost every night, unless we have somewhere to be, we spend our time hanging out watching TV together and talking. There is no place I would rather be than with him, and I think this has been paramount to our recovery and will continue to be important to our future together.

FINDING YOUR TRIBE

The interesting thing is that while I was making these changes for Superman, I also felt a sense of relief. I spent a lot of time trying to make everyone happy, which included never saying no to doing things I did not want to do. Now, there was a legitimate reason for us to take a step back and make a new short list of what we liked to do for fun, and who we liked to spend our limited time with. We started making plans with other couples that like to play games. I am fully aware that this is nerdy and will delve deeper into our transformation into our parents shortly, but for right now, I am talking about restructuring our entertainment. We went from meeting couples in restaurants and sharing bottles of wine, to eating at my house, having a nice home cooked meal or ordering in, and breaking out a good old-fashioned board game.

This was when I started to realize that what I used to enjoy doing was no longer fun to me. I do not want to wait hours for a table at a popular restaurant every weekend. We would end up spending hundreds of dollars on food and alcohol when we would have a better time ordering in with friends and playing games. And we have discovered that most of our friends love a good board game. We just had to find our new tribe. Your tribe is the group of friends you have who share interests, make you feel included, and think you are "normal."

I recall when my son was an infant, maybe a year old and able to sit up, I noticed him taking the corner of his play mat, lifting it up and putting it down repeatedly. I started wondering if he had autism. Why was he doing that? Shortly after that observation, I noticed his little buddy, on his own mat, mirroring this peculiar behavior. I no longer find this odd but deem it as "normal."

Asking ourselves what is normal and what is not is a question we all ponder multiple times a day. Ultimately, we seek out others who normalize our feelings and behaviors. When someone makes us feel like we are weird or less than, we shy away from them and seek out like-minded people, and they become our tribe.

When I was anorexic, I sought out others who found calorie counting, picking at food, and obsessing over exercise normal. Adults who like comic books go to Comic-Con. People who like to play bridge join a bridge club. Golfers get tee times to wake up at the crack of dawn to meet others who see nothing wrong with the insanity of hitting a ball into a hole.

See how this goes? So, where our evenings used to be about food and spirits, they shifted a little. Now the focus is on friends and fun.

This experience made me look inside myself to determine what I did out of obligation versus what I did out of desire. While I am curious about many things, the few things that I do not waiver on are exercise, reading, music, and watching T.V. I also happen to be obsessed with my Peloton Spin Bike. This is not a sales pitch, but if you do want one, my referral code is MGVH8S. This bike has helped me in so many ways. In a nutshell, Peloton allows you to take a spin class taught by an instructor in the comfort of your own home. The bike is top notch, the instructors are the best I have ever experienced, and the community is like my second family.

For those who do not know about Peloton, we are viewed as a cult. However, the members are the most incredible community I have ever stumbled upon. I have met some of my favorite friends through riding together and meeting in the main studio. Peloton also has Facebook fan pages. Stop laughing, yes there are fan pages. This community is really supportive. We all have a passion for riding, the brand, and its coaches. Only if you drink the Kool-Aid will you want to talk about the bike ad nauseam as we do. The bike has removed the anxiety I had around not being able to get to the gym with my schedule. It also ensures that I get a really solid workout every day. The community part was a benefit I did not see coming but readily welcomed. If that is not your cup of tea, no matter. There is another tribe for you, and it is worth finding.

A DOG WOULD HAVE BEEN EASIER

I had the hardest time with this chapter because I do not want to give fodder to the inevitable therapist my son will be seeing when he blames his life on Superman and me. There are a few things for which I would love a do-over. I am sure there will be many more, but the biggest regret I have is his diet. The theme throughout this book has been my hang-ups with food, my weight, and exercise. Knowing that I was preoccupied and had issues with food, I was clear that I did not want to do the same to my child. I was so happy that he was a he because I think I would have had a harder time with a girl and her weight.

I decided to allow my son to eat when he was hungry and not make a big issue of food. He also dictated what he liked and did not like. This was fine until he decided that anything green was poisonous and that he only like fried foods, macaroni and cheese, pizza and garlic knots. He is a little on the heavy side, but even more disturbing to me is that his diet is far from balanced and entirely comprised of processed foods. I am subtly trying to undo what I did, but it is a struggle. I hate to put this on his future girlfriends, but that is where we are at this point. I wish I could fix it on this end, but it is very difficult to reverse.

I also did not want him to stress the way I did over grades. Well, it worked. He could truly give two shits about his grades. He is completely happy to simply pass a class. If he had challenges learning, that would be one thing, but he is smart and capable. Instead, he is very lazy and uninterested. I waver between thinking he will snap out of it and praying that he will be drafted by the Yankees.

When he started school, I envisioned us sitting at the kitchen table while I helped him with his homework. I would recall everything I learned with ease, and he would be grateful that I was so smart and willing to help. Reality check: apparently, what I know is outdated and irrelevant. I recall one time, when we were working on math, he informed me what I know is now called "Mom and Dad Math." How I learned to do math is not part of the Common Core. Simply stated, what we learned is now useless. Rather than expressing gratitude, my son shows no patience, is annoyed that I am not up on current teachings, and he is downright nasty. My response is equally nasty, often reminding him I already passed school. I tattle to Superman, and my son decides that doing the work independently and not passing would be more pleasurable than working with me. Realizing that someone could sustain an injury, I hired a tutor. A no-nonsense tutor, who is disciplined, serious, and not me. Therefore, sonny boy is on his best behavior, and I do not need extra hair color to survive. To his credit, since transitioning from elementary school to junior high, he does not ask for assistance. He does get decent grades on his own without much help from either Superman or me. I do not see him spending a lot of time on schoolwork, which has me a bit perplexed, however, out of sight out of mind is my motto. I am not anxious to relive the early days of doing homeworking together, so if it ain't broke, why fix it?

Today's kids seem very self-indulgent and entitled. I am guessing every parent makes this observation about the new generation. Parents are mostly to blame. In this day and age, kids do not have to earn things. They simply whine and are appeased. I remember having to save up my allowance and babysitting money to get the latest craze. Now, at least in my community, kids are given things as soon as they come out, really to stifle the nagging. This is a poor anecdote and not teaching them how to prioritize or handle money. Yet, I am also guilty of indulging him, because it is easier. I criticized how frugal my parents were, but in retrospect, I am so happy with what I learned from them. While they were extreme, it was made abundantly clear to me that if you cannot afford it, you do not buy it. Many of my peers are not good at budgeting, so they are in credit card debt. I self-talk about working on implementing some sort of change to how rewards are obtained for my son, but somehow resort back to old habits because I have to pick my battles.

I did not realize how self-centered he was until I tried to take him with me to the Homeless Coalition, where I volunteer. We spent a few days, painting, sorting donations, and stuffing backpacks filled with school supplies for kids who could not afford them. Expecting him to be filled with gratitude and understanding, I asked him what he thought about the experience. He replied, "it's not really for me." Floored, I asked him which part, the helping people or the physical labor? Thinking it is the age, I still expect him to acknowledge the privileged life he has been afforded. He is an only child, and it has been our joy to give him things that we did not have when we were kids. He has enough signed sports memorabilia to pay for his first year of college. He has been in the Legend Suites at Yankee Stadium, met several Yankees, and has been taken to places my husband and I would never have dreamed of going when we were kids. I think since this is all he knows, and some of his friends have similar lifestyles, he does not think any of these amenities are that big of a deal.

When Mother's Day and Father's Day roll around, I expect an outpouring of love and gratitude for being such amazing parents. So far, this has not happened. Or I guess it did happen, but Superman and I praised each other. Our son did not even give us handmade cards. I wish I held back on the gifts and let him "earn" things. It is a disservice to excuse him from helping around the house and contributing to our household. I am feeling exceptionally under-impressed because he just had a very average report card. He could have done better if he tried harder. It is hard to explain to a pre-teen why learning about volume, mass, and other uninteresting extraneous facts are necessary to succeed in life. I too remember questioning, "what am I going to do with this information?" However, at his age, you do not know what will pique your interest hence reveal your career path. Therefore, it becomes important to learn that sometimes we all have to do things we do not want to do, but you have to learn discipline and responsibility. He is not going to have the lazy summer he anticipates. This is when being a parent is more crucial than being a friend. I hate it, but I will do it. Just another phase that seems so hard to manage, but you make it through. Despite his apathy, there have been flickers of a moral compass that give me hope. He has heart, and when push comes to shove, he does the right thing. He shares and is sensitive to other people's feelings. Awareness comes with maturity, and this is all part of the process. I continue to remind him to always pay it forward and try to recall what I was feeling at his age. I do think it was all about me. Understanding where I am now, I am confident this is a phase.

I'M SO SORRY

Mom and Dad,

I am so sorry I never hung up my coat when you asked. I never walked the dog or took out the garbage. I never cleaned out the hutch like you asked. I left my dishes in the sink. I put all of my stuff on the dining room table despite your requests to put things away. I never offered to help when it would have been super easy.

I asked for many things thinking that others got more. What I got was far greater than material things, and I am so happy that you frequently professed your love to me and I reciprocated when I was old enough to appreciate the value of these words.

You taught me how to manage money. All of those years that I thought you were so frugal, and you were, you managed to teach me the value of saving and not living beyond my means.

You taught me to always pay it forward and to laugh every day. You showed me what love looks like with your enduring relationship and gave me something to strive for.

You constantly reminded me of what was important and not to be so materialistic. I am not sure that fully worked. I do like my things. I wish you had splurged a little more on yourselves, and I constantly question why my sister hoarded ketchup for years, and I cannot stop buying paper towels and toilet paper. Was it because you said it is stupid to run out of things? Or was it that we only had one of everything? I cannot recall. I sometimes laugh when Superman sees something deteriorating, tells me it is perfectly fine, yet I immediately revert to Amazon to replace it and restock whatever we are talking about. Somehow, I think this is from you, Mom and Dad.

MY PANS ARE ALL BURNT

When I think of my parent's kitchen, several vivid memories come to mind. The first thing is the cereal cabinet. They had a pantry filled with ten boxes of cereal. They ate cereal every morning with freshly percolated coffee. They mixed a couple flavors. The gross part is that many of these boxes had bugs. Apparently, this is not uncommon, but I find it repulsive nonetheless. I determined they were Indian meal moths but knowing their name does not make it any less disgusting. So, we have that. Next, I recall a can filled with grease which smelled horrible. The purpose of this can was to prevent the grease from going down the drain and clogging the sink. They would pour the grease into a tin coffee can, and when it got full dispose of it. If you can imagine walking through a restaurant kitchen that makes a lot of fried food, you will have a good idea of what the kitchen smelled like. My favorite item in the kitchen was the table which we were allowed to write on while we ate. We used to play hangman and other games during dinner, and it was really a unique way to connect during meals. I am reminded that there were ants around the sink, and a sponge that was so old it was a quarter of the size of a normal sponge, but they liked to get their money's worth.

The reason I bring my childhood kitchen up is that when I envisioned what my kitchen as an adult would look like, I imagined copper pans hanging from the ceiling, lots of light, white floors and flowers everywhere. Every night I thought there would be a picturesque meal, similar to those you see in a Martha Stewart magazine. Fourteen years later, I am going to tell you that all of my pans are burnt. They are not pretty. In fact, they are pretty ugly. The reality of those kitchens that you see on *Fixer Upper* is that they have not been used. If you actually apply heat to your pans, they are not going to look pristine. Especially if you are running late and do not take the proper time to warm the pans up gradually. If you are in a rush and put the burners on high, your pans will look like mine. Next, if you place them in water while they are still hot to prevent the food from sticking to the surface, they are going to warp. These are my pans.

It is not rare for my smoke detector to sound when I am cooking. Nor is it odd for me to melt some sort of plastic, like a chip clip or a spatula on the stovetop. Once in a blue moon, a magnetic clip will find itself stuck to a baking sheet and make it into the oven to wreak havoc. Where I used to be so upset by a mess or not having everything in its proper place, I have learned to embrace the homey feeling that comes with a little disorder. My house often smells like food, but that is because I often cook. I take pride in serving my family homecooked meals. I knew that I did not want my son to feel like he could not live in his own home. Do not think the thought of crayon on my walls did not enter my mind, but I knew I wanted his memories to be of a welcoming home where he could invite friends.

It took me a long time to be able to actually use things rather than save them for a special occasion. I still do not eat off my Ralph Lauren wedding china, which is stupid, but I am not there yet. However, I do wear my good jewelry daily, and I do not save my shoes for special events anymore. I want to get joy out of my possessions. I learned this after watching things that I cherished go out of style before I even took the tags off and that is a great lesson to have embraced.

WHEN THE SHIT HIT THE FAN

Thinking about my life thus far, I cannot believe how quickly time passes. Sometimes I actually forget that I am not in my twenties, but if I forget my body reminds me on a daily basis. The purpose of reflecting on the different obstacles you conquer over your lifetime is to learn how to handle situations better. You might hope to recognize what is really important and what is just wasted energy. I wish I could tell you that is how I am embracing menopause, but I would be lying.

I am furious that all of a sudden, I have mysteriously put on weight for no good reason except I that I am old (ish). I feel like my clothing got tight overnight and my body parts started shifting, drooping, and puffing up so much I feel like I could deflate myself with a pin. I actually crackle when I get out of bed. I feel victorious when I wake up, and my knee does not hurt, or my neck does not have a crick in it. I was thirty just the other day. Then I stop and remember that was almost twenty years ago.

My sister warned me about her weight gain, and I have definitely heard other women complain, but I truly thought that because I was so active, that somehow this would not happen to me. I assumed that their diets got sloppy or they stopped exercising. This is not the case, and I feel a bit guilty that I thought they were to blame. I am definitely ten pounds heavier than I was last year, but I eat exactly the same, and I exercise the same amount, if not more. I was so upset I started running on the treadmill with a weighted vest, hanging from pull up bars, wearing a booty belt to no end. Not only was I giving myself injuries, but I was not making any gains. Well, I was making gains, but not improvements. Weight gains.

A 2012 study in the *International Journal of Eating Disorders*, found that thirteen percent of women over fifty exhibit some related symptoms such as binge eating and/or purging, extreme exercising or excessive dieting. I agree and think it could be higher. I would not want to revisit having an eating disorder, but I am so unhappy about this weight gain. It becomes even more challenging for me because comparatively speaking, I am still thinner than most of my friends. When I complain I am not fishing for compliments, I can assure you. I am truly upset over my new norm. While some say they do not see it, I feel it. Whether it is visible with clothes on or not, the number on the scale does not lie. My tight pants and much larger chest make my clothes uncomfortable. That is my reality. I am careful not to talk about my weight with others who are struggling, but it is on my mind, and I am trying desperately to get a handle on the weight gain. What used to work is no longer effective. Typically, I do not stop until I get what I want within reason, however, I am not sure what else I can do that I have not already tried. The best would be to fix my head, but it is hard to teach an old dog new tricks.

While I do not binge-eat because that would make me feel guilty and I do not purge because that is just gross and not as easy to do as you might think, I do exercise ad nauseam and think about my calorie consumption all day. I once again worry about socializing around food and try to figure out how I can still enjoy myself while not beating myself up over a changing body that is almost out of my control. I constantly wonder how other women grab appetizers that I want but do not fit into my allotted calories for the day. When I eat a big meal and plan to eat less later in the day, I worry about how hungry I will feel. This is still diseased, but who I am. Why don't others feel the guilt like I do? Or do they, but make a conscious choice to ignore the negative feeling and indulge?

Another new symptom I thought was contributing to my clothes, not fitting was the fact that I started having trouble going to the bathroom. I was very regular for years, but then suddenly, I did not have the urge to go to the bathroom. I started to worry. Where was all of the waste going, or I should say, not going? I confided in a friend who is going through similar issues. We actually call or text each other for weekly fat talks. Sometimes we just text each other with an emoji of a pig nose. That is enough to convey the disgust we feel over our current weight. I asked her if she had any suggestions that may rectify my rectum. She wrote back almost instantly with a remedy. It was something called Cleanse More. I read the ingredients, and they sounded like they were all herbal and no harsh chemicals. I thought it would be worth a try. So, if this book becomes a hit, people are going to be really disgusted by this next tale and perhaps not look at me in the same way. However, if that is the case, I will most likely be rich, and I will just buy new friends. Conversely, if this book is a bomb, then no one is the wiser, but it is too funny, not to share.

I got my Cleanse More from Amazon, so I could have it in a day. I took the pills and assumed that when they kicked in, I would have a normal bowel movement. Well, I am claiming the term "shit happens" as my own. This story is horrible, especially because it happened to me. When I woke up, I had no rumblings or any urge to use the bathroom. I thought perhaps because it was all natural, maybe it was not strong enough. I put it out of my mind because I had to catch a train into the city for a work meeting.

Once in the city, I hear some growling. This is not going to be good. I start to panic. If you are not aware, there are a lot of people in NYC. This makes it next to impossible to find an empty bathroom. I tell myself this is not happening and get through my meetings, trying to ignore what is going on in my body. I know I have to do whatever I can to get the hell home. I made one attempt to go to a remote bathroom in a restaurant that I thought might possibly be empty. To my dismay, there was a lady by the sink putting on make-up for what felt like an hour. I was sweating profusely and wanted to scream, "get the hell out of here, it is not helping you." Then my boss walked into the bathroom, so as an excuse to be there, I washed my hands. When I exited, I was still in no better shape than when I started.

We continued to Penn Station and then take off in different directions. She goes to NJ, and I head east, so I thought I was in the clear. It turns out, however, that she had a few minutes before her train, so she decided to look for me. At this point, I am ready to pass out, and I decided to go into the bathroom at Penn Station and pray no one will figure out what stall the fumes are coming from. I had no other choice. So, I go in and let me tell you I wanted to put caution tape across the door. It was BAD. I felt so much better, but I was afraid to come out of the stall. I waited so no one would know it was me, but when I came out, I noticed several women giving me the STINK eye. I totally deserved it. There was a mass exodus.

A little while later, walking around the station, I run into my boss, who had come down to meet me, and she tells me she had to leave the bathroom because a homeless person shit the bathroom. I resented that comment, I have a home, but I am ninety-nine to one hundred percent sure that I was the culprit.

I resolved to never ever use that cleanse again. I had gotten another recommendation from a different friend called Super Dieter's Tea. What could tea possibly do? Here is the answer, it can do a lot. This next episode happened on New Year's Eve. I recall it because I was taking down my Christmas tree ornaments. I thought maybe I will have a cup of tea to make some room for Hibachi since a few days had gone by since I had defecated, and we were going out for a big dinner to ring in the New Year. I drank the tea at about two PM, which was totally STUPID. It says works within five to seven hours.

Anyway, we went out with a bunch of people to Hibachi and, as the chef is putting pounds of butter onto the grill, my stomach starts to gurgle just watching. We make it through the meal, but before we can head to the next destination, I tell my husband I have to go home immediately. I begged him to go through red lights because I did not think I would make it. The moral of the story is Super Dieter's Tea needs to be consumed near a bathroom, preferably when no one is home.

After that, I called my gastroenterologist to tell her about my problem and to make an appointment. I bring my cleanse, my tea and a few other laxatives that I tried when I could not take it anymore. I thought I had made very natural choices and that she would applaud my efforts. I dump my bag and her face crumpled. Instead, she told me, "no, no, no, no. You are going to have a lazy colon." I wanted to yell, "lady nothing about me is lazy," but I listened. I made an appointment for a colonoscopy.

The preparation for a colonoscopy is the worst. You have to take laxatives and drink a ton of MiraLAX, which thankfully I could mix with Vitamin Water, so it did not taste too horrible. And then I spent the entire night shitting my brains out. Of course, this experience was miserable, but I was looking forward to weighing myself in the morning even if the loss was water weight.

So, after a night of explosive fun, I weighed exactly the same. WTF? How is that even possible?

As I am waiting to have the procedure, I am on the table, and the anesthesiologist (who was a woman in her fifties) asked what brings you here? I tell her about my constipation and weight gain, and she said, "Honey, that is menopause." I wanted to punch her and cry simultaneously.

My new morning routine involves taking twelve pills, to make sure I go to the bathroom, keep my memory intact, and move my joints. I even started eating prunes.

Aside from the fact that these changes are uncomfortable and inconvenient, I also find them depressing. To me, they prove that I am no longer young and there are going to be more ailments creeping up that seem inevitable. I am sure watching the decline of my parents and my mother-in-law have not helped me deal with these feelings. Again, since the alternative is definitely worse, the only option is to handle the changes with grace and enjoy everything, but when you feel bloated and hungry, it is hard to celebrate life.

THE STINKING TRUTH

Another disturbing thing I have noticed is that I do not smell as nice as I used to smell. I am assuming that the combination of supplements I am taking produces some odd odors. I am now very diligent in safeguarding against "old people smell." When you are younger, and you think old people smell, those old people are in their fifties. Now that sounds middle-aged to me. At first, I denied that these odors were coming from me, but then I noticed after a regular workout, I was totally drenched, and I stunk. Considering I was in the basement alone, there was no one else to blame. At first, I thought my sports bra was too old, so I tossed it, but I do laundry every single day, so it is not like the clothes sit in sweat long enough to sink into the fabric. Tossing it out did not resolve the problem. I am the problem.

Unpleasant odors must be another side effect of stupid freakin' menopause. Since my son plays video games downstairs where I work out, I literally spray air fresher every twenty minutes, so he does not think he has a smelly mom. While on the topic, my pee is not smelling that great either. So now, I am spraying everywhere and rubbing fragrant creams on myself multiple times a day. Brushing my teeth after every meal and frequently checking that I smell like lotion. I always showered every day anyway, but now sometimes I shower more than once a day.

If you have XX chromosomes, you better check your pits.

MOM, WHAT ARE THOSE LINES ON YOUR FOREHEAD?

Out of the mouths of babes. Or rotten teenagers in this case.

I have noticed, thanks to my son, some fine lines, that are getting finer by the year. I would never have paid attention to them, except people keep pointing them out to me. I met a woman while I was trick or treating with my son, who sold anti-aging skincare. We were talking and really hit it off. Then she started telling me about how she got out of corporate America and was riding the anti-aging wave. She floored me when she told me how big the market was, and later, I went home and looked in the mirror. I am not sure why I never noticed my wrinkles, but I am guessing it was because I was preoccupied with my weight. However, now since she brought them up, I am sort of obsessed with them. She looked fantastic, so I said to myself, "I'll have what she's having." Now morning and night I slather myself with anti-aging creams, retinol, and things to minimize sunspots. I roll my skin to stimulate collagen growth, and I actually sell the products now to get a discount. My husband is using them too. He has never looked better, so I am glad I did not even have to ask him to try. He must have admired how fabulous I was looking and got curious. However, he now takes longer in the bathroom than I do.

TO PEE OR NOT TO PEE

Next, I started to notice that I could not make it through the night without getting up two or three times a night to pee. Which was not the biggest deal when I was suffering from insomnia but led to waking up tired. So, I had to see what I could do to remedy these new symptoms as well. I was so tired I considered sleeping in the bathtub, but that is just disgusting.

I went to a urologist and then proceeded to make an appointment to have a urodynamic test. I had no idea what I was in for, but this glamorous test involves a catheter. You sit on the commode, and they fill up your bladder to measure the flow of your urine to see if you are emptying your bladder. Sort of humiliating, but the end result is that I needed to have my urethra stretched.

WTF, I am only in my forties. The tail end, but still. This is not giving me a good feeling about the future. So yes folks, I go and stretch my poor urethra, but I am wondering, since I am now drinking gallons of water, to flush out my fat cells, how is this going to work? Trust me when I tell you, it did not tickle, but the end result was good.

I never really had trouble falling asleep, but for some reason, I was starting to have problems being able to sleep through the night. Clearly peeing every two hours was not helping, but I got that resolved, and I still could not sleep. I tried Melatonin, but that was for novices. I now take Magnesium and Sleep Aid, which is Melatonin plus, and I sleep through the night. Ideally, I was always one to discourage taking anything that contained a drug but being sleep deprived for so long changed my opinion. Sleep is necessary, so if I need a little help, then I am going to take it.

I know more is coming, I have not even gotten to the hot flashes yet. I do have to color my hair, but at least I have hair. I know that some women notice thinning hair and others find hair growing out of their chin and on their toes. So not glamourous. A friend of mine told me something that happened to her when she got her indoor spin bike. She said when she first started riding the bike, she was in tremendous discomfort and she attributed that to the seat. It is really common in the first few weeks of spinning that the seat hurts. So, she ordered padded shorts, tried putting maxi pads in her underwear, and lifted and lowered the seat to no end. She decided maybe she should consult a doctor to make sure nothing else was going on. Wouldn't you know it, vaginal dryness. You guessed it, "Sally, this is just one of those things that happens to your body during stupid freakin' menopause." So, she started taking oral estrogen pills, which gave her yeast infections, UTI's, and dermatitis. I do not even know what that is, but any "itis" is not good. Finally, she found a cream that she has to insert up there twice a week.

So, to recap, I am heavier, I smell, I have insomnia, and I pee every hour on the hour, I have wrinkles, gray hair, and am sort of moody. Maybe they should call it Menapplause? Do they deserve applause for sticking with us?

What do they get? Perhaps a lower sex drive and trouble getting an erection? Big Freakin' Deal. For some stupid reason, men have a longer shelf life than women. Their beer bellies seem much more acceptable than our muffin tops, and when they go gray, they look distinguished. When we go gray, we look old. What a double standard.

I am trying to find the silver lining, but youth really is wasted on the young.

TRYING TO FIND MY WEIGH

I have probably not missed a workout since I was fourteen. I mean even when I had bunion surgery, I bought the dumbest machine ever, called an Upper Body Ergometer. This was the worst Christmas gift I have ever picked out for myself. I just knew that during my recovery, I had to do some sort of exercise, so I would not put on weight or get soft. This machine was basically a treadmill for your arms. You have likely seen a hamster doing the same motion. I did the machine forty-five minutes a day. I think it burned 104 calories. Basically, about five croutons.

My typical workout schedule is usually six days of cardio a week, most sessions sixty minutes or more and then I sometimes throw in Pilates, or a walk with weights and I personal train clients, which sometimes leads to extra working out. Since my body has gone into hibernation mode, I could triple my exercise, and I do not think it would make a difference. I am sure you know that if you go from doing nothing to something, the results are much more evident that if you go from just trying to work harder at what you are already doing. I could up the exercise, eat less, drink gallons of water, take fat burners, eat spicy food, but weight gain is pretty much hormonal and out of your control.

I wish I did not care, but when your pants are tight your day sucks, it is just a fact of life.

Ten pounds may not sound like the end of the world, but my clothes do not fit, and I just look different to myself. My bras are not closing, which may sound like a nice problem but, remember I am in the *National Geographic* phase of things, also known as the pigmy look. In fact, I was at a party having a fabulous time when, all of a sudden, my bra popped open amidst a crowd of about three hundred. I tried to subtly re-hook it, but it just looked like I was feeling myself up. Not the best way to make a first impression. I managed to escape to the bathroom, but where did these torpedo tits come from?

I went to get some new sports bras from a store that I regularly frequent. I proceed to the dressing room with my usual size medium, put the bra on, and discover my chest is definitely bigger. Now I am stuck. No, I mean really stuck. My arms are twisted in such a way that I think the bra is going to rip. I am all alone, but my boobs are sticking out, so I cannot call for help. I am laughing and crying at the same time. I take a few deep breaths, and after a good ten minutes, I am out. I felt like Houdini. Apparently now I am *large*.

My pants do not fit either, and my shirts resemble belly shirts. I resolve to get a new wardrobe rather than start every day in a bad mood. It is funny, but I remember as a child cringing when I watched my mom getting dressed and saw her skirts all seemed to have elastic and safety pins around the zipper. I just thought she was, well cheap, and weird, but now I know, she was dealing with the mystery weight gain too. Sorry Mom!

Sometimes I reminisce about the sexy lingerie that I used to wear when Superman and I started dating. There were French maid costumes, thongs, lacey peignoirs, really nice stuff. Now, I have a huge over the shoulder boulder holder with granny panties.

Trying to figure out how to get this unavoidable bulge gone...

I decided to try a high-end nutrient dense plant-based meal delivery plan. Thinking this plan might be the answer, I had renewed vim and vigor. I learned about the program through a friend who tried it, and then again from an exercise instructor I follow. The food is beautiful, comes with love notes, and flowers, and costs more than my car payment. But again, can you put a price on your health, I ask you?

I ordered a one-day trial for one hundred dollars. This order was only for me, so Superman and the kid were on their own. They would not be able to live off plants alone anyway. In fact, my son will not eat anything green. Not even for money. I have tried. Getting back to the food. The way it works is you pick a day of three meals or three meals a day up to five days a week. The menu is set, you do not have choices. I panicked when I saw what I was getting since it included "Beet Rawvioli." I was not a fan of beets. My husband and I tried going raw for three days, and we ended up on a seven-day steak binge. So, I tried to get ahold of customer service. They only provided an email address, but through ways, I cannot reveal, I uncovered their phone number. The woman inquired as to how I got the number, I told her not to worry about it, I have a bigger problem, I hate beets, so you have to help me switch my dinner. She assured me that this meal is a little slice of heaven and to have faith. I hesitantly hung up thinking I just wasted a hundred bucks but resigned myself to the loss and went on with my day.

The food arrived the next day, and when I bit into the Rawvioli, I actually think I heard birds singing. Holy shit was this food amazing. I could not believe it. Since I am a bit of an extremist, I started to wonder what I could pawn to get more of this amazing food. This food was going to solve my issues. I decided to look at their career section to see what I could do in exchange for food. Don't you know it, I started to write for them in exchange for food. I could not be happier. It was a dream come true since I love to write, and now I had access to this fantastic meal plan.

The company is a bit bohemian and way more relaxed than I am. The arrangement was I would write two articles a month for two full days of food. That is equivalent to two hundred dollars. I was so excited that I pumped out ten articles in a week. The company rarely stuck to the deadlines, and I found myself waiting for them to publish, but they all made it. It was going so well until the Editor fell in love and decided to leave her job and make jewelry in Hawaii. I had hoped that her predecessor would keep me on, but they ended up pulling all content in house, and I had to pay for the food. I was back at the drawing board yet again. I am not going to lie, as much as I loved the food, eating plant-based was very challenging for me to do all of the time. I should have seen the writing on the wall when I started adding chicken and croutons to the food.

My next idea was to enroll in an accredited nutrition program. I thought if I could understand the science behind my body, then maybe I could figure out how to tweak my diet and get a handle on my love handles. Stupid name, who loves them? Muffin Top is not any better. Is that supposed to remind me that eating muffins is how I got here in the first place? So, I voraciously scoured the notes, watched the webinars, and homed in on any information that could help me decipher the code.

I did not find what I was looking for, so I decided, with my investment, I was entitled to correspond with the teacher directly. When I did not hear back, I went full force and posted my question on her Facebook page. "No one puts baby in the corner." Well folks, I do not think you are going to like her answer any more than I did.

I would like a refund.

Simply stated, she said, "You don't look like you did when you were thirteen or twenty-five, this is just the next phase of the lifecycle."

Not gonna lie, I wanted a pill, a game plan, or some sort of anecdote. Her response was depressing and not very motivating, to say the least.

SELF-INFLICTED MIND GAMES

There have been some survival tactics that I have embraced to help me combat my battle of the bulge. These allowances help me mentally, but I am not sure if they have any validity.

In my demented mind, I have deemed certain foods as acceptable even though I know they have no nutritional value and are pretty high in calories. For some bizarre reason, these specific foods do not make me feel guilty. Like for example, frozen yogurt is total crap, but I think because it has the word yogurt in it, I am good with it. Then I top it with chocolate covered pretzels, trail mix, and banana chips. Let's dissect: chocolate high in sugar, pretzels white flour, no nutrients, peanuts and raisins okay I could make a weak argument for, and deep-fried banana chips? But again, there was a banana used in them, so I am good with it.

Still confused? Okay, take a muffin. I would never eat a chocolate chip muffin, but I would eat a reduced fat blueberry one from Dunkin Donuts. Yup, I am not kidding. Furthermore, I will drive to the Dunkin Donuts that puts the sugar on top because they taste better, but because they are reduced fat, I can rationalize this choice. There are many more that I have managed to accept such as sugar-free vanilla creamer, which I know is laden with chemicals, but somehow okay in my book. The best one is any type of salad in a taco shell. Everyone knows those shells are deep fried, but yet I still work with the salad part and I manage to eat the entire shell and do not feel too badly, usually. See the salad negates the shell.

Most of the time, I eat very healthy meals, but these are my acceptable cheats. I really resented when restaurant menus started listing calories. That is just so damn mean. Especially my favorite salad from the Cheesecake Factory. I made up the calories based on nothing but a number that would allow me to eat it without guilt. When the real number was revealed, I was off by more than four hundred calories. I did not stop eating it, I just felt shitty. Was that necessary?

It is very difficult to decipher what is true and what is just marketing propaganda. These messages sometimes pray on the fact that consumers may not truly understand what is being communicated, and what is a credible source and what is not. Not to get too scientific, but if you know anything about food, your goal should be to eat non-processed, whole nutrient dense foods. This is supposed to help with satiety and your overall health. Which leads me to another pet peeve. Supposedly, foods that are high in nutrients are supposed to be more filling. I find this to be bullshit. I want that to be the case so badly. Badly enough that I have ordered another meal replacement shake that is supposed to be delish and fill me up. This is going to be the third shake I am trying, but on most days, I want the shake with my meal rather than as a replacement. I try to bulk them up by adding Cacao Bliss (which contains superfoods) PB2 (high protein peanut butter powder with less fat) but in all honesty, I just really want a buttered bagel. I am just letting you know you are not alone in your closet love for carbs. I am right there with you.

It also annoys me when other people profess that these drinks and bars fill them up. Maybe I am actually missing a gene or something. I am very rarely full. That leads me to the second question that I brought up during my nutrition class. I detailed my diet to the teacher and explained that I am often not satisfied. The teacher suggested that perhaps I was misreading my cues. Perhaps I was thirsty rather than hungry. I am close to fifty years of age, and I am pretty sure I know if I am thirsty rather than hungry. I am just Hangry (Hungry and Angry).

Superman suggested I just make a bunch of new heavy friends and wear leggings. I think he is really sick of my complaining and I cannot blame him. He stumbled upon something called SculpSure and shared a video with me. I was wondering if he thought I was getting pudgy too, but I pushed that thought to the back of my head and watched the video. I also read about a hundred reviews, and seventy-six percent of them were positive. I was nervous, so I called my best friend to get her opinion, and as it turns out, she had scheduled a consultation for a similar procedure called Cool Sculpting. Getting her buy-in convinced me this was the way to go, so I booked my own consultation and I was elated. I was going to laser my fat cells away once and for all. My clothes would fit, and I could concentrate on bigger things (or hopefully smaller things).

When I called SculpSure, I explained what was going on with my body, they took my measurements and told me I was the perfect candidate. I did not want to chicken out, so I asked if I could have the procedure done immediately, on the spot. For three thousand dollars, they said, "we can squeeze you in".

The way I understood it is that this particular procedure was for people who lived healthy lifestyles, ate relatively clean, and exercised. It is designed to target trouble spots that are not responding to exercise. Once there, I put my laser belt on and laid down on the table for my twenty-five-minute procedure. All belted up the quadrants started to heat up, and it sort of felt like my skin was going to melt off. I told myself it is only twenty-five minutes. Thinking I was about fifteen minutes in, I asked how much time had elapsed, and the assistant said it had been about six minutes. I really wanted to cry. IT HURT A LOT.

After the procedure, I was not too uncomfortable. Well, that is compared to my skin burning. My instructions for after the procedure were to drink a ton of water and massage my flanks. So, I was drinking gallons and massaging daily. I waited the twelve weeks and went back for my second procedure. They begin by opening my file and telling me that I actually looked like I put on a few pounds. Now I am upset, the technician calls in the head guru, and they huddle together. When they were done talking, they tell me I need to go up to 1.4 and the Diamond. I have no idea what this means, but it sounds serious.

I thought I remembered the pain of the first procedure but reminded myself that it was only twenty-five minutes. This time I brought music to listen to during the procedure. I thought that this would provide the distraction I needed to endure the pain. Well, it started out fine, and then it got so hot that I actually pulled my earbuds out and asked does anyone not finish the session? The technician said I have not lost anybody yet. I am too competitive to be the first quitter, but tears were coming out of my eyes. I think it may have felt worse than labor. Somehow, I made it through. I was thinking this would be a perfect punishment for terrorists.

I didn't notice any change after all of that and my friend, who did cool sculpting, did not notice any results either, and her treatment was even pricier than mine. I am embarrassed that I went through with it. I would not be if I noticed any improvement, but currently, I just feel like a sucker. What I am noticing, is that by sharing my tale, I am getting feedback from women who have had similar experiences, which again just makes it feel more normal.

DANCING WITH THE OLDIES

If I am ever able to justify doing a Richard Simmons workout just stick a fork in me. I will officially go over to the dark side at that point. I will carb load, change my name, and relocate.

I do want to acknowledge that regardless of how determined my mind stays, my body is lagging behind. At least in my case, my workouts are different then what they were in my thirties.

I constantly make an effort to challenge myself, and keep changing up my workouts, so that my body does not get used to my routines and no longer makes improvements. I have noticed as of late, that whenever I try something new, I seem to end up with a new injury. My last endeavor was a class called *Surfit.* Why would I think I could do this, considering I have never stepped foot on a surfboard?

The class takes place in a studio where that are several surfboards situated on top of three secured stability balls. Clearly, making balance challenging. Thankfully, I was alone on my first attempt, which was good because I could get personalized attention, and bad because I could not duck out. I was doing surprisingly well until the instructor added plyometrics. Typically, I can do either cardio or strength training, not both simultaneously. I need to totally focus, so when the movements got explosive, I lost my rhythm, and all bets were off.

Same issue happened when I tried TRX, I ended up with some knee pain. I wish I could say it is because of my form, but I have many degrees in training and am very conscious and careful with my positioning. It is basically from four solid decades of working out intensely. I have not looked back since I was fourteen. I am so grateful that I am able to spin twenty miles a day, and lift weights, run on occasion and continue to personal train several clients. I have noticed that I am slowing down though in terms of my stamina and ability to incorporate new disciplines.

MANY NUMBERS TOO LITTLE TIME

Trying not to feel discouraged that I am not performing at the same level that I used to, I started to think about what I am hoping to accomplish. If age is just a number, and it is not how much you weigh but how you feel, why are we married to these awful numbers that someone decided defines us? I do not have the answer. I am just asking. I was thinking about it this morning: Kids have to get over a sixty-five for a passing grade. I have to hit a certain cadence and tension to get to a certain output on my bike, so I feel like I had a good workout (no regard to the fact that I am red as a beet and cannot breathe). I have to make a certain salary to consider myself a success. I want to fit into a certain-size-jeans before I am happy. Who determines what a size four is? My waist is not changing, but I could wear different manufacturers and span from a size four to a size eight in the dressing room. Four makes me happy, eight makes me mad, and I am the same size regardless of what the label says. Not to get too philosophical, but sometimes I think the numbers make us mental.

I do think in general people need structure to make them feel secure. I love having goals, especially so I can blow by them. However, when they are not attainable, they have the opposite effect. I have noticed that I am not as literal as I used to be in following these proposed guidelines, mainly because there are too many of them. How do we determine what parameters are important enough to warrant caring about them? For example, I do not suggest you read this and then ignore your blood pressure or LDL cholesterol. Those numbers are important, but I have been hung up with turning fifty, even though I have only been forty-nine for a minute. Age is just a number, I feel fantastic, and according to Superman, I only look forty-two. So why can't I stop thinking about turning fifty?

Different people need different things. Some people need to be accountable, and numbers give them a goal. Others, like myself, obsess over getting to specific suggestions without considering the feelings. What I have just discovered through writing is that I need to concentrate more on how I feel rather than hitting a prescribed goal. Words to live by!

A friend clued me in on the principles that teachers are encouraged to adhere to:

SMART stands for

- Specific,
- Measurable,
- Attainable,
- Realistic/Relevant
- Time Bound

I love thinking about letting go of the numbers. Can I do it? Can you?

WHO NEEDS ANCESTORY.COM?

I know from my guilt over everything that I must be Jewish and Italian. I feel guilt at least fifty times a day. Guilt over exercising too little, guilt over eating too much, guilt over not getting enough accomplished in a day, guilt over not separating my colors from my whites, guilt over not cleaning up the house, guilt over spending too much money, guilt over not eating organic. I could keep going, but I think you get the idea. Is this learned? Does everyone face the same level of these self-deprecating unproductive feelings? How do we learn to be kinder to ourselves?

I am in the middle of a bout of guilt right about now. There was a trigger. I was up to my usual Saturday routine which involved errands, a manicure and of course a personal training session. At the last minute I decided to change into some jeans since it was pouring outside, and I wanted to put on rainboots. Granted not a great choice for workout gear, but I am the trainer, so I do not usually do a full workout, but rather demonstrate what I would like my client to do.

My jeans split in half. My granny panties were hanging out. Not only was I embarrassed, but immediately I thought to myself, I have no business being a trainer. How could someone with my body be considered a professional giving advice? GUILT! The funny thing is, if I had been younger, I would have run home and changed immediately, but the older version of me was too practical. Instead, I tied a sweatshirt around my waist and proceeded to get things done, so I did not have to backtrack. I made it through my obligations, got home, and showed Superman my mangled jeans.

He said exactly the right thing, "that is poorly made material and clearly defective."

Kudos to Superman. I have him well trained, and he did sound sincere. I asked myself, what could I change to make myself feel better?

I feel like I am going to be plagued with these feelings of guilt and despair until I figure out how to get back to my old fighting weight, which does not seem possible. It might be possible if I started eating air again, but I am thinking to myself I do not want to go back there. I may have been thin when I was eating clean and too little, but I was not happier, I was just thinner. Just to add insult to injury, I wore a pair of shorts today that I knew would pop a button at any time. I just could not part with them until that became a reality. Today was the day, but my plan was not the best thought out. I did not consider when and where I would lose *said* button. It happened in the deli, and I almost lost 'em. The challenge was carrying my salad and phone up to the counter while trying inconspicuously to hold up my shorts. They were old shorts. I know I should be okay with it, but the reality is, I am not.

I am just waiting to wake up to how I used to be, and it is not happening.

I'M NOT MOODY, I AM COMPLEX

Actually, I am moody, and maybe I always have been, but what I am finding is that I am less inclined to hold back my displeasure and adoration in the same vein. So, when someone pisses me off lookout, but conversely if someone helps me, I want to acknowledge it and host them for dinner. I really have been happy for the majority of my life. I find joy in very simple things, but lately, I find myself irritated over stupid things that I cannot let go of. Here is an example: if I get takeout and the order is wrong, I am irrationally mad. Like big deal, they left out my croutons. However, to me, this is a crime. Not only will I call and get a credit, but I demand a formal letter of apology. Well, actually, up until this minute, that had not been a consideration, but that is going to be added to my compensation. I am pretty sure it is hormonal, but let's be honest, if you are someone like me who spends a lot of time and care trying to do everything right, at a certain point you realize that you are alone in your quest for perfection.

I feel lately that most people just do not give a shit.

I have a hard time understanding this apathy. I care deeply about everything. I try very hard never to cancel plans. Obviously, things do come up, but I have been on the opposite end of this equation, where I am excited for something that is coming up, only to learn that the wind has changed direction and the plan is not happening. I invest way too much emotion into things of this nature, and I seem to feel it more the older I get. I would have thought the opposite to be true, but not the case.

I am also disappointed by how much effort it takes for me to get up and out. When I hear of an opportunity that sounds like fun, I immediately say YES, which has been my response my entire life. Lately, I start thinking about how tired I am going to be in the morning. When did I become such an old fart? When they say you do not recover like you used to, it is no joke.

I took my friend out for her fiftieth birthday the other day, had one glass of Moscato and woke up a moron. I had such trouble getting out of my own way. I was tired, had a headache and felt lazy. It was one glass. I had a wonderful time, but the next day I was a bag of shells. What happens to our stamina? Is it just me? I used to not eat, smoke pot, go out until the wee hours of the morning and still function like a champ. Now I have one drink, and I function like a chump.

This has happened more than I would like to acknowledge, but this is life in the fast lane.

I used to love cooking dinner for my family, but after fourteen years of cooking approximately five nights a week, it gets tedious and boring. My son has a very limited palate, so automatically, I am making two different dinners. Before you roll your eyes, I acknowledged that I f'd up. I was liberal because when I was a kid, I hated having to eat what was on my plate. Now, I wish I had enforced eating what is on your plate like my parents did to me. Then you have to be imaginative, so you do not make the same food week after week. I do not know what I would do if I had not discovered Blue Apron. The only issue is, I still have to make the recipe. This is a meal plan that comes weekly with recipes and ingredients. I spend a good hour every morning, chopping for the evening meal. It is a pain in the ass. When they come out great, I am proud. When they are very bland and not worth the work, I am angry. I am always tempted to get takeout. Then I think, in this order, I am fat, it is a waste of money, and I just have to get to Friday, and I get a break. That is so lame, but that is what is going through my mind.

I am way more energized in the morning. So, after I get out of the morning haze, before the fog is back, I chop everything that I may need for dinner, make lunches, workout, and by 9 AM. I have done most of the irritating things of the day. I tell myself I love working out, but that is a little bit of bullshit. The truth is, I love how I feel after the workout is done, and I have showered. I love that I can eat more or have given myself permission to eat since I burned calories, but as I am sweating and challenging the limits of my endurance, I am not having the best time ever. The best time ever is usually watching TV with my husband eating takeout.

For some amazing reason, I am never or ninety-five percent of the time not moody with Superman. He brings out the best in me and is so even-keeled, I aspire to have an equally level disposition around him. When we are alone, this is not difficult, sometimes my son will bring out my anger, but it is short-lived.

FIGHT OR FLIGHT

Fear apparently has no age. The only thing that changes around fear may be your coping mechanisms and your self-judgement. I have many fears that I fight. One of them is traveling by myself. I think this stems from my horrible sense of direction. It really could not be any worse. I always walk the wrong way first. Good for getting my steps in on the Fitbit, but otherwise frustrating. I can get lost using a GPS if you can believe that. I totally thought I was pulling off how bad my directional skills were until the other day, Superman suggested I study a map. I said something that he would have made fun of to me if someone else had said it. You do not get to know what I said. Sorry, not sorry.

He is right. I cannot be mad either, it is embarrassing.

One time I was going to a nutrition summit, which I was privileged to be invited to. It was in NYC, at my favorite haunt. It started very early, so I had to catch a seven AM train. I had some coffee, lots of coffee as a matter of fact. As I got to the train, I realized I forgot my license, my credit card, and was unsure of which subway to take. That panicky feeling started to take over my thoughts. I did some self-talk which really does help, but my heart was still racing.

The older I get, the less I like crowds and people for that matter. I like my little bubble, so my words included how much this was an opportunity to learn and be around people whom I admire. I had mapped out the route, and let me be transparent, this was not my first or second time to the destination, I just usually go with others and follow the leader. Although I try to remember the route, it seems to go out of my head as quickly as it goes in. Of course, it is a Sunday, and the subway that I have taken in the past is not running. There are hundreds of people to ask, and I do, and I find it.

I get there right on time, and my breathing returns. Now I am amongst a group of equally enthusiastic fans (I should say fanatics), but I do not know them.

I start mingling, but as I do, my thoughts are racing. I think everyone looks better suited to attend than I do. I think everyone is prettier, and all of these negative thoughts enter my mind. I am faking confidence. Then we do a group exercise which involves sharing vulnerabilities. I learn that I am surrounded by people who feel the same way. This repeatedly floors me and makes me question why we are all so insecure. After all of these years, those raw feelings come to the surface in a heartbeat. Is that innate or learned? I think it is a combination of both.

From talking to many friends and acquaintances no matter how confident you come across, there seems to always be some insecurities lurking just below the surface. My parents played everything safe and were very cautious. I tend to strive for the comfort zone, but also have tremendous FOMO (fear of missing out), so I push myself to the edge more often than not. I would say nine times out of ten, I am grateful that I did.

I study people who seem more at ease in situations that fluster me. I have a friend who travels for work every other week by herself. She goes to other countries and does not worry about anything. I wish I could imagine doing that, but I cannot. I get anxious just thinking about the airport. She does not show fear over much, but there must be something.

I know one of my anxieties that developed over traveling started around food and exercise. I was so rigid with my routines and schedule that traveling would get in the way of my rituals.

I have overcome the fear around food, but I still feel it around working out. Once again, Superman knows this about me and works with me to let me get my exercise in.

This is so necessary for my mental health, and I am beyond grateful that I can share my idiosyncrasies (or crazies as I like to call them) with him and he does not judge me, but instead helps me figure out how to manage.

I am not sure about where my fear of not looking attractive comes from. I do not look in the mirror and think I look pretty. I never really have. Sometimes I think I look good, for me, but that is as far as I go. I have received many compliments in my life, but I usually rationalize that people think I am nice, and therefore, it makes me more attractive. I think this is a problem, and I do not really understand why I feel this way, but I do. It is hard to talk about because I am not fishing for compliments. They are true feelings, and they hurt. They have lessened for several reasons. My husband has done wonders for my confidence. Do some people not struggle with these insecurities? I do think most of us have them. He tells me I am beautiful, and I believe he means it. I try to visualize what he sees, but I cannot. However, I really do care about being beautiful to him, and this has helped me tremendously. Looks happen to be my insecurity, but I have friends who have not gone to college who think not having a college degree defines them. Or others who defend their jobs, because they do not feel proud of where they are in their lives. It would be much more useful to think about what we have accomplished as opposed to where we feel deficient.

I have discussed my body dysmorphia with people who I would kill to look like, and they start picking on themselves too. Why do we do this to ourselves? We are so blessed to be healthy, and I get annoyed with myself for how I constantly criticize myself, but again, I move forward and try to change my self-talk. It does make a difference. The interesting thing is, some people fear things that I never worry about, which I find fascinating. Here is a perfect illustration. If I am going to the city to present data to a client, many would panic about the presentation. I barely prepare for the presentation, but I do a trial run to get to my destination because I am not convinced that I will find the building. Logistics are my issue, the content, I can wing. I have always been able to succeed at presentations, so that is a secondary concern.

I have another fear that seems totally irrational even to myself, but it is real. I have panic attacks over snow. Here is the dumbest part. I work from home. I have a gym at home. If it does snow, I do not live in a desolate area, I will be dug out within a day. So why does snow freak me out? If I had to guess, it is linked to my fear of not having control. Maybe I will not be able to drive? Maybe my plans will get canceled? Is that the end of the world? It most certainly is not, but it literally causes me to have panic attacks. My heart races and my thoughts run wild.

I am old enough now that I can work through it, but I wonder why I am wired this way. I do think it is innate since my siblings do not have the same worries. I marvel at the people who dig themselves out and go to work as if it is no big deal. I worry. I worry about Superman. I worry about the bus my son takes to school. I worry about me, although I am not moving out of my chair. Feels nutty.

Here is another great example. My colleague is a world traveler. She has been to several countries, navigates airports and customs with ease but will only get into a taxi, never a subway. I always take the subway, and I should be fearful because I am generally relying on tourists and strangers to tell me if I am getting on the right one. I just do not want to pay for a taxi. I wish I did not waste so much time worrying. It has invaded space in each phase of my life. I wonder if there is any benefit to worrying? I guess it keeps therapists, hair colorists, and doctors in business. I do feel accomplished when I conquer a fear or do not let it get the best of me. At least I wish it would speed up my damn metabolism, but in reality, I think it just produces cortisol, making my gut thicker, and turns my hair gray.

Lastly, what comes to mind is how quickly one worry can supersede another. I recall how I used to ruminate over the care of my mother. I do not want to say I forgot her, but after I had a baby, caring for her was not as daunting as my new fear of taking care of my infant son.

How much fear do we create for ourselves?

REUNITED AND IT FEELS SO GOOD

I actually went to my ten-year, twenty-year, and thirty-year reunion. I had a surprisingly good time but was amazed at the anxiety I felt about attending. All of those insecurities that I faced during high school seemed to come flooding back. I was definitely less concerned by the thirtieth, but it was interesting to see who showed up, and what cliques still existed. Believe it or not, some were still intact.

I think some people show up to say, "look, I made it." I get that. Others are oblivious to the struggle that others face during adolescence. Someone who I considered a bit of a snob back in the day was there, but I went up to her to say hello anyhow. She asked me, "who are you?" I gave her my name, and she said, "no, I don't remember you." Interestingly enough that was at the twenty-year reunion, but by the thirty-year reunion her amnesia seemed to dissipate, and not only did she remember me, but recalled that we were buddies. A classmate of mine who lost her battle with breast cancer, actually posted on social media before she passed, that she wished she had been nicer in high school. I bring this up because I wonder why some kids are accepted and accepting and others ostracized and outcasts. Is it our peers influencing our actions? Our parents? Do we follow along, so we are not the targets, and why does history repeat itself?

When I was discussing this with my sister, she suggested that it is perhaps dictated by who you hang around with. However, I was in a pretty popular crowd, but I never felt like I belonged. Not because of how they treated me, but by how I felt about myself. I was actually not genuine about wanting to be there. I think this is one of the benefits of getting older. It is nice to be at an age where you don't give a shit about what other people think of your choices. I am actually there.

I did a lot of things that I did not necessarily want to be a part of. Several crazy Manhattan nights, parties, clubs, dates and other social activities that were not really of interest to me. Why did I go? I went because I wanted to be perceived as popular and in the right crowd.

In retrospect, there were probably some really great friends that I missed out on because I wanted to look cool. I was not ever mean, but I was not always true to my heart.

Those high school cliques continue throughout life. You have sororities and then the damn PTA. I wanted to be in the PTA, not going to lie, until I went to the first meeting. I actually went to a few, and despite my desire to be there for the benefit of my son, I decided in this scenario, cash is king.

It's the oldest story in the world. One day you're seventeen and planning for someday, and then quietly and without you ever really noticing, someday is today, and that someday is yesterday. And this is your life." — Nathan Scott

OMG, I AM TURNING INTO MY PARENTS

Honestly, I cannot believe it. I really thought I would always be current, cool, and in the know, but I am starting to think I may be wrong. I first got concerned when I walked past a window, saw my reflection, and immediately went into a panic. First, my pants were so short, if I did not know it was me, I would have yelled out, the flood is over. It gets worse. With those ridiculously short pants, I had on loafers with socks. I cannot explain why. Did I black out when I was getting dressed? I asked the friend whom I was with how to fix my fashion catastrophe. Quickly she advised me to ditch the socks, rolled up my jeans, and just like that I course corrected. This was an eye-opener.

How many other things have I had on that I should not have worn? I do understand how this happens. Some of the clothes that used to be so cute and appropriate, do not fit my new lumps, and just do not look the way they used to look. Sometimes I put something on thinking that I can definitely pull it off, but maybe I cannot. I have seen some people who think they can pull stuff off, and really should have reconsidered.

The other habits that just sneak up on you are gradual. So be warned.

I do not take sugar packets home, but I do take home salad dressing. If I find a good one, I ask for an extra. It is not just me either. I had dinner with a friend last night, and I asked for a side of goat cheese for my salad. They gave me the goat cheese. There was a lot leftover. After the meal, we were getting ready to leave, and she had the cheese wrapped up along with the bread basket. Apparently, the cheese was for me, which I did not want. When I let her know that I was not going to take it, she became incensed and a bit frightening. I capitulated, and then she confronted me and asked if I was going to throw it out. I could not lie, so it ended up going home with her.

It just happens.

My parents were the extreme. I do not think I would, put ketchup on pizza, because I did not have an open bottle of Ragu. I would not use Ragu in the first place. I would not freeze a sandwich from Subway, nor would I eat onion dip that was rained on. However, I do try to use everything up in the fridge, even if I do not like it.

I find myself playing board games like they did and doing puzzles. My mother loved a show on PBS called *Upstairs Downstairs*, which I thought was beyond boring and totally for old people, yet it seems very similar to my beloved *Downton Abbey,* which I binged watched and cried when it was over.

I am big on coupons and read in my free time, just like they did.

I am more of a homebody than I used to be, and neither my husband nor son like to go very far either. My parents loved being home too.

I used to love going into NYC, but now I find it is too crowded and cannot wait to come home.

As my parents used to say, "if you're not early, you're late." Needless to say, I am always early.

As I get older, I seem to be doing all of the same things that I used to pick on my parents for doing.

Sometimes I watch the Billboard or MTV awards, and I do not recognize a damn song. I tell my son his music is not real music. You cannot even understand the lyrics. Now my radio is tuned into Yacht Rock (similar to easy listening, which used to make me cringe). I watch the news which I could never understand. I floss, my teeth, which I used to fight doing. I did not realize how conservative I have become, because it has been gradual, but I am starting to see the similarities.

There are a few things that I have not inherited. They used to sit in the last row of every play or concert or venue we went to, to save money. Thanks to my husband and my poor eyesight, we are always far forward. We go gambling without guilt, and when we go away, we always stay in very nice accommodations, rather than their preferred Howard Johnsons. We spend money on our home and fix all things immediately, but that is my Type A personality rearing its ugly head. I do have high-end taste, and I know my father would not understand the way I spend money, but he also grew up during the depression. I do not want my money to be spent on a nursing home. I certainly learned from them to never live beyond my means, but conversely, I know I cannot take it with me.

Thanks to good financial advice, my mother's monthly rent was paid for by her Medicare. You need an advocate when you are unable to live on your own. Unfortunately, if you do not plan ahead and act proactively, you could end up running out of money. The elder lawyers and administrators of these facilities do not make it easy. We were very lucky that my sister was well versed in estate planning. Having watched what went on with our mothers, just reinforces the fact that I want to enjoy the money while I can, and not spend it on exorbitant medical costs. If you do your due diligence and prepare, you should be covered by the insurance you have paid into for your entire working life.

I think in regard to my husband, he has always been an old soul and since both of our parents were older when they had us, we are melding into a version of the parents from *Leave it to Beaver.* I am actually happy about this transformation. What used to be "cool" to me, is immature now, and I am grateful that I am following in the footsteps of a couple (my parents) who had a beautiful lifetime love affair. I am not ashamed to tap my foot during a musical and talk to strangers in the supermarket. These are the things that make me smile when remembering my parents

NERDY IS MY COOL

A wise man once said, "I am too young to appreciate doing nothing." That man was my thirteen-year-old son when asked if he wanted to join us on a scenic boat ride while we were on vacation in the Poconos.

I am thinking about this, after a night out in a club dancing, and seeing a band. I was very conflicted when I came home because the event triggered a lot of feelings for me. First, I recall how going out at eleven o'clock used to be the norm, and now, I am yawning at ten PM waiting for the closing act and praying there is no encore.

As I look around, I make several observations:

- There is a lot of plastic surgery going on, and it does not usually improve the situation. Note to self, no matter how good the infomercial seems, remember SculpSure.
- I felt self-conscious about my dancing. I watched others and sort of judged them. I thought they looked a bit foolish, but they were just having fun (if I am judgy it is because I am watching, which means people would be watching me too).
- The judgment part really was only around the ones who had too much to drink and were purposely trying to attract attention. The highlight of the night occurred when one of the "show-offs" tried to recreate a scene from *Saturday Night Fever* but tripped over her own bag which she put on the floor.

My friend and I high fived each other when we caught each other chuckling as she tripped.

Sometimes when someone addresses me as a ma'am, I question if I should go under the knife. I will never say never, but right now, I doubt it. In my opinion, from what I have seen, it is always obvious when someone has had plastic surgery, and you cannot defy time. The wrinkles that you earn are a sign of where you have been. Of course, I do everything I can to diminish signs of aging, but if we could look at them as a badge of honor rather than a sign of being put out to pasture, we would not only save a ton of money, time, and negativity but we could concentrate on making the most out of every minute we have left.

What I realized is that my party scene just changed. The party went from dancing and the bar scene, to book clubs and game night. While I felt nostalgic in one sense, I am relieved that I do not have to do what I perceive to be as cool. I am an adult who can make choices, and furthermore know what I like to do.

I do not like places that are prone to people getting drunk and knocking into me with no remorse. I do not like having drinks spilled on me. I do not like the smell of sweaty people in close quarters.

I like to go to bed by eleven.

Spending time with the people I consider to be my "lifers" is what I enjoy doing. Talking, laughing playing games. Nerdy is my cool.

One of my greatest pleasures is my book club. The story of its formation goes like this. I was taking a spin class on a consistent basis, where I became friends with a woman who was an avid reader like myself. She had just read a book and was raving about the story. I immediately got the book and devoured it cover to cover. When I saw her again, we got very animated talking about how great it was, and she asked me to join her book club. This was like making it into a sorority to me. I came home, practically skipping. It was winter, so the book club was not due to gather until spring.

Finally, it was time. When I get to the gym, my friend tells me that she will call me with the address in the afternoon. I did not leave the phone for one second. It rings, and...

She regrets to inform me that the consensus was that there were too many members in the book club already and that I was un-invited due to overcrowding. She felt terrible, and I knew it. I said it was not a big deal, but I was crushed. As I mulled it over throughout the day, I went from sad to angry.

Finally, Superman said, just make your own damn book club. The wheels started turning, and my competitive nature sprung back to life. I was determined to make it better than any book club out there, whatever that would mean. I emailed an author and asked her how much it would cost for her to come to my house. She politely told me that I could not afford it, but she would be happy to Skype. Thus, the Condon Book Club was born.

The first meeting, I went a little overboard served sushi and about fifteen other things, and it was a huge success. I was elated and could not believe my good fortune. I had a face to (digital) face dialogue with one of my idols. This became the norm for two years, until the authors started coming in person, or inviting us to restaurants, and treating us to meals.

The author who did the first Skype with us hosted us at her country club two years later. A day I will treasure forever. This was a perfect example of how to make lemonade from lemons.

YOU CAN'T ALWAYS GET WHAT YOU WANT, BUT IF YOU TRY SOMETIMES...

I want to start out by saying this next tale is not my fault. Clearly, I could do better at letting things go, but when I feel that an injustice has been committed, I must advocate. As evidenced above by the book club, I do not like feeling that I have been slighted.

You know how many ads we are all barraged with over the holidays. My rule of thumb is one gift to give one gift for me. Thanks to business intelligence software, every single suggested post is something I need. In this case, Moncler gloves from a website in Italy.

An important lesson I have learned is to stick to domestic purchases.

They were expensive gloves, but I was in the holiday spirit and decided that if I made an extra sale at my job, it would cover the gloves.

I cave and order them, without paying much attention to the details. Now I am really excited, and when I get the tracking number from DHL, I follow them online as my gloves get closer to my door.

They come at night, as Superman and I are watching TV. I tear the box open, and they are beautiful. I remove the tags and immediately put them on. They feel really big, but I try to ignore the fact that I cannot feel anything because there is so much extra material. We pause our show so I can look a little closer at the tag and realize that I have purchased men's gloves.

Now I am in a panic, I try to roll them up to see if I can get them to feel more comfortable, but I am no large man. I decide to write an email to the company and explain my faux pas and hope to exchange them for a smaller size. In the meantime, I go to the site, print out a return label, and pack them up. I did have Superman try them on, and he was not impressed with them at all, nor would he wear them. Now I am even more determined to get them back. I look up the number of DHL and schedule a pickup. I feel anxious, but the plan is in place, and at nine-o-one AM I will be on the phone with DHL, and I will get the right gloves. So, Superman and I finish our show and go to bed. I cannot wait until morning, so I can fix this situation.

I wake up and as soon as it is humanly possible, I contact DHL to schedule a pickup. Feeling all wound up, I get on my spin bike and try to dissipate my anxiety. DHL comes, and the gloves are back en route to Italy. Suddenly an email lands in my box from the website stating, "we are very clear about our return policy, and unfortunately if you have removed the security tags which validate the authenticity of said gloves, we will not be able to process your return."

Their email made me crazed, so in typical Laurie fashion, I first ask Superman, and then a bunch of other people if this seems just. Of course, everyone thought this was ludicrous, but because the company was in Italy and the gloves were already heading back there, I could only express my disappointment via email.

I reply to their email, "I have had the gloves less than twelve hours, and furthermore, I do not make fake gloves in my house. They are the exact pair that were sent to me. I do not want my money back. I just want a smaller pair. You will see all of the tags are included in the designer bag in which they arrived."

I wait a day, thinking, the department that handles returns will see that the tags are intact in the box, the gloves are pristine, and they will just process the return, and this will go down as a lesson to me.

I receive another email, stating, I am sorry that you are disappointed, but we will be sending the gloves back to the original address. We cannot process your return.

Now I am furious, and start to rant, "Superman, can you imagine that they think I am sending back fraudulent gloves?"

He confirms that I am in the right, and it is ridiculous. To pour salt on the wound, they have signed each email, *at your disposal.*

I write back again, "if you were really at my disposal, you would help me, which I see you are not willing to do. I am contacting the credit card company."

I get Capital One on the line, I tell them my story, and they transfer me to the claims department. I do emphasize that it is clearly stated that the tags must be on the items for a refund. In my head, I thought I told them the tags were in the box and could be easily reattached, making this is a moot point. Capital One said that I did not have a valid claim and that I should contact PayPal. UGH.

So, now determined that I am going to fix this, Superman starts watching a show that I do not like, and I start my defense. I call PayPal, and get Betty on the phone, and tell her my story. I reiterate to Betty that I am an honest person, and I did, in fact cut the tags off in my excitement, but the item does not fit. She empathizes with me, and says, we could say that they do not fit the description on the website, but that is not true, and I determine I am out of luck. I want to have Betty over for dinner, but I needed to figure out my next moves before making dinner plans.

Nowadays you must have receipts to get credit, so I have a brainstorm. I google the number to Customer Service at Moncler. I am sure when they see how their distributor is treating me, that they will do the exchange and perhaps reprimand the company for poor customer service.

I craft my email and feel a sense of relief. Assured that I have come up with a resolution, I feel a sense of calm wash over me. Of course, this has been going on for a solid week, and now we are about one week out from Christmas. People are going to start their vacations.

I go into DHL tracking and see that the gloves have been received and I am hoping that a credit will be issued and that when Moncler contacts me, I can say this has all been resolved. Now it is a Wednesday or a Thursday, and I get my fourth email from the distributor, saying that very shortly I will be receiving a tracking number for the return of my return. I decide, I better send some more emails to Moncler in case my email did not go through. I send another five emails feeling that someone with a brain will rectify this situation, and I will laugh about it in the near future. I hear nothing through the weekend, and now it is Christmas Eve. I send my tenth email, and now I have contacted some Moncler stores in New York City to see if they could do the exchange. Of course, they respond by saying we cannot exchange an item that was not purchased from this particular store. I drop some science on them and remind them that they can sell them, and I could potentially become a worthwhile customer since I am a shopper. I mean I bought these online from Italy. I am a great potential buyer. They could not see this from my perspective. They did not have the gloves in stock anyway, so I proceed with more emails stating how I have been wronged that I am incensed that no one is getting back to me. I have left messages, and written emails to at least ten people, and I did not get one reply. I feel completely ignored. A few hours go by, and I get an email from the Assistant to the President, stating that they cannot interfere with one of their wholesalers, but they have a similar return policy, and the tags must be intact.

Now I am crabby, pissed off, and out of luck for the moment. I am also anxious about hosting Christmas. I am really only used to cooking for three or four people, and I was having seven. Not only was I stressed about making sure everything came out right, but I have just discovered that one of my guests has allergies so pretty much everything on the menu was going to be an issue. I talked to the guest, she made some of her own food, Christmas morning was a success, and the meal came out fine. I tell the story of the gloves Christmas morning, and my tribe insists that I will find a way. At this point, I am not so sure.

In the meantime, I get a nice new Fitbit and charge that baby up and enjoy the days off that follow. As I look at the metrics on my new Fitbit, I notice that I have done 11,000 steps and it is saying I am only at about two miles. I have been wearing a Fitbit for three years, so I know 11,000 steps is over four miles. Not to worry, I call the Fitbit hotline, and proceed to measure my strides and do a factory reset. This takes over an hour, and I am sure that my next workout will have the right metrics. I should mention, that because Superman and I compete over who gets the most steps, I wear the device on my ankle because it does not really track the bike activity as steps when it is on your wrist.

So now it is day two, and I check again and see that my 10,000 steps have only yielded .6 miles. I quickly call the hotline, and they walk me through a few troubleshooting steps and determine that I need to send it back.

Now I have men's large gloves and a broken Fitbit. Not good.

I drop the watch off at FedEx, and I am told I will have a new one within two weeks. Since I am in a bitchy mood, I call back and say it is not my fault that you sent me a broken device, I think you should overnight me one that works. I get put on hold, and they say you are right, we would be happy to accommodate you.

Fantastic.

Wait, there is a slight problem. The slate grey you ordered is back ordered until March, but we do have burnt orange.

I reply, "of course, you have burnt orange because no one wants that color." I continue probing to see if I can find another model in a better color. I am, of course more agitated now, because of the whole glove incident. I am feeling that Santa has me on the naughty list. It turns out Fitbit makes a version of the watch I had just gotten with a few extra features, but it is about thirty dollars more. I said I want that one for my troubles. The customer service rep said she understood, but they could not make that exchange since the items were at different price points.

I let her know that she was very lovely, but now I needed this escalated to a supervisor. I am put on hold once again.

She comes back on the line and tells me that it has been approved and that they will be sending me the higher end model at no extra charge.

I am very pleased and thank them profusely.

The rest of the week goes seamlessly, and I did enjoy the rest of my vacation. DHL comes knocking, and I sign for the floppy gloves I had returned. I try them on again to see if they had shrunk.

They had not.

Next, I start googling Department stores that carry Moncler. I proceed to call all of them to see if I can arrange an exchange.

After an hour worth of phone calls, I think I find a store.

I put the gloves in a gift bag. The Distributor reattached the tags, so now I have my gift bag and I go to the counter and explain, "My husband got these gloves, but he doesn't appreciate them, and I would like to exchange them for a women's pair." I am feeling like a criminal, and I am just waiting for security to arrest me. I am sweating, and I cannot stop talking, although the associate had already left to get a pair of women's gloves.

The women's pair is $245 more than the pair I was exchanging, but at this point, I felt I deserved a four hundred and fifty dollar pair of gloves and I exchanged them. Walking out, I felt victorious. The associate got a sale, I got gloves that fit, and they were after all genuine and re-sellable.

I get back to my desk, and my answering machine is blinking. I play the message, and it is Morgan the store manager of the Moncler Prince Street store and she has been informed about my situation. I feel obligated to call back. She did leave me her cell number, so I get her on the phone. I tell her of my trials and tribulations, and she tells me to hang on to her number in case I have any other needs in the future. I also told her I felt guilty, but she assured me that I did nothing wrong. The next day, my phone rings, and I recognize it since I dialed it so many times. Yes, it is the Moncler corporate headquarters in NYC. Jennifer got my message and had been out with a stomach virus. I proceed to tell her my tale, and she advises me to keep her number in case I have any other issues.

I am expecting a coat to arrive in the mail any day now.

It is not about the money but about the justice. I was trying to explain this point to my handyman Fidel. His second language is English, but he pretended to understand what I was trying to convey. I told him, I love paying him, because he works so hard and his work is so good, he deserves the money. I just do not like being taken advantage of or being treated unfairly.

I am pretty sure he did not understand my story, but he gave me a "si, si," which is what I needed at the time.

I am feeling good about everything now, but I am sure there will be a part two to this book since I have a lot of life left, so Moncler better keep that in mind.

YOU KNOW YOU ARE GETTING OLD WHEN???

Last week, I went to my son's baseball game, and the next night while we were sitting on the couch watching TV, I noticed my elbow was very sensitive. I showed my elbow to Superman and asked him if it looked questionable. He pretended to look, but when he is engrossed in TV unless it involves doughnuts you have to wait for a commercial.

I figured I must have hit my elbow on something and put it out of mind. A few days went by, and it was still bothering me, but now it was red and sort of hot. Suddenly, my family started treating me like I had the plague. Of course, it was the weekend, because it is always the weekend when you need your doctor. So, I was forced to go to urgent care.

Urgent Care really has been very good every time I have visited, but I am always skeptical of their expertise since they cover all ailments rather than specialize.

I see the doctor, show him my elbow, and he advised me that it is either bursitis or an infected bite. That is a very wide spectrum. He prescribed an antibiotic and told me to follow up with a hand surgeon who also handles elbows. This is when I dismiss him in my mind. Why would I need a hand surgeon? Sorry Doc, I was wrong. Even so, I did what he said and called the orthopedic surgeon's office on Monday but made the mistake of diagnosing myself with a spider bite and conveying this to the receptionist. She informed me that this would not be the appropriate office to visit.

I started taking the antibiotic, and multiple times a day, I stuck my elbow in people's faces asking them to diagnose it.

I do not recommend asking people who are not doctors.

I was told I had lime disease, I could go septic, it was a spider bite, and that I could lose the arm. Now I am freaking out, but it is after five PM, and I am forced to call the emergency hotline.

I tell the operator the story to relay to the doctor. I am waiting and waiting, and then my internet goes out, which causes my phone to go dead. My head is racing.

Finally, the on-call doctor gets through, I tell her the entire story, and she eases my mind. She switches my antibiotic and advises me to bust into the office the next day whether they can squeeze me in or not to have an orthopedic surgeon drain my elbow. I really was anxious, but I felt like I had a game plan, so I made it through the night. I go to the appointment resigned to the fact, that I was going to have a needle stuck into my elbow. I was dreading this procedure until I meet the doctor, and in a very arrogant way, he writes on a napkin olecranon bursitis.

He proceeded to tell me that I do not have a bug bite, and he cannot help me. I must have looked like I was doubting him because it was itchy, but he said there is no question that it is bursitis.

Now I am begging him to reconsider and stick a needle in my elbow. He replied this is not his expertise and recommended another practice. I asked him what causes this pain, and the first thing out of his mouth was AGE. Now I hate him. I got teary. It is exhausting when you feel like no one cares, and you are not getting anywhere. I called Superman, and he actually came home to check on me. That made me feel a million times better. I called the original office that I had called on Monday (it is now Thursday), and lucky me, I get the same girl at the desk. She remembered the call. That does not surprise me because

I must have sounded like a lunatic. She gets me in the following Tuesday. As I anticipated, this was where I should have gone the Monday after Urgent Care.

I get my elbow drained, and all is back to normal. I was given an anti-inflammatory which upset my stomach. However, it did not go to waste since Superman woke up with a stiff knee from sleeping. So, he made use of the medication. We both wake up, hobble downstairs and take our pill regimen that is sort of nauseating. When I start getting melancholy, I think of my mother's famous line, "think of the alternative," so I swallow the tablets and thank God for my good fortune.

IS IT WORTH IT?

HOMEOSTASIS

The *Webster Dictionary* defines this as "the tendency toward a relatively stable equilibrium between interdependent elements, especially as maintained by physiological processes."

I woke up trying to understand how we determine what has value. This has always been of interest to me from the time that my beloved father said to me, "why do you spend money to have someone paint your fingernails?" He was truly at a loss. My retort was, "why do you spend money to hit a ball into a hole for an entire afternoon?" Of course, I was referring to golf.

We are constantly deciding what is worth spending our precious dollars on and what is not. Believe it or not, I have linked this back to anxiety. Talk about having an overactive mind.

A scenario came about that I used as a teaching moment. It makes me vulnerable to share it, but I did already tell you that I was constipated, had an eating disorder, was molested and split my pants while training someone, so I guess I should not bother getting self-conscious now.

In this case, I had a conference coming up in Brooklyn and had recently been reminded that Brooklyn is part of Long Island. For some reason, I thought it was part of Manhattan. Clearly, it is a borough of

Manhattan, and you take a bridge, aka the Brooklyn Bridge to get there. I just never really put thought into it, but I am guessing I will never forget that fact again. Anyway, I have a very limited area in which I feel comfortable driving. We have established I cannot find my way out of a paper bag, I cannot see very well, and I sometimes get road rage. Therefore, before I booked my ticket to this Nutrition Masterclass, I asked Superman if he would drive me. He assured me that it would be no issue, book away.

So, without further ado I reserved my fourteen hundred dollar ticket, and booked my thousand dollar hotel room for the three nights, knowing that I was going to be living the dream (my dream, I know that hanging out with food obsessed, fitness zealots might not be everyone's nirvana).

Fast forward three months and now the trip is one week away.

I remind Superman, who is beyond stressed out because of some complications at his job. He nods his head, but I have been living with him long enough to know that I need to find a ride.

My first feeling, after the anxiety, is anger. When I bought the ticket, he assured me he would drive me there, but now I was going to be left in the lurch. The reason I share this intimate fact is that I uncovered the rule to a good marriage while thinking about this situation. I think it is a teaching moment for me to share and remind myself of its importance. If I was in any sort of life or death situation, I know Superman would be there unequivocally as evidenced by many tales thus far. He works in finance doing the budgets for a multi-billion-dollar company. It was the height of his busy season, and we are not poor. Why wouldn't I think to just take a car service from the get-go? It is because I have a hard time placing value on taking a car service to my destination when we own two cars. What I failed to place a value on was his time.

I could feel his tension and was worried about his well-being, so I sent him an email because I like homeostasis, and I was feeling that our house was out of balance. I indicated that I was concerned about his stress level and offered to help in any way to ease it. He replied that he was going to send me in a car to Brooklyn because he could not leave to get me there.

That makes total sense, but I instantly felt hurt yet relieved. Let me dissect.

I was hurt because he said he would take me, and once again, I am stuck figuring out my own dilemma. It did not feel like a partnership. However, when I stepped back, he offered me an alternative. He came up with a solution that would work for both of us. I realized that my ask, although at the time several months back, was not selfish, became impossible for him to carry out. The resolution was provided, and he offered to pay. So why did I take this personally? And furthermore, why did I spend two thousand four hundred dollars with ease but not want to pay a hundred bucks that would not only alleviate my worry but also eliminate a burden on Superman?

As soon as I spent the time thinking it through, the problem went away. I averted an unnecessary fight and reminded myself that I was too consumed with my own shit and was not being a considerate wife. Superman's mood was markedly improved, and my anxiety was gone after I walked myself through my feelings. I often consider why I got so blessed with an amazing marriage, while others around me are unhappy and complacent with their marriages.

That example I just provided is why. Sometimes, you have to rationalize the irrational thoughts you have going on in your head to figure out where they are emanating from. I long to be taken care of by someone. I am taken care of when I need to be but think about how hard it is going from being a kid with no responsibilities to becoming an adult with every responsibility and then some.

I always asked my parents to drive me places, and they did. Naturally, I still wanted to ask them, but the difference is I am an adult, I have money, and now I have a resource to call. That peace of mind and mentality are priceless. What has to be the most valuable commodity in your life is your relationship. Ever since the time that the security of my marriage was threatened, I step back and evaluate. This is why I am able to cherish every day that I have with my best friend and husband.

Of course, I did talk this through with my friends before determining if I was going to be mad. One of them shared a conversation that she had had with a co-worker. Her colleague frequently came home from her big job as a CFO to find her husband watching *Law and Order*. She immediately felt resentful with good reason. I do not think that men and women have equal roles. I think a lot of shit gets dumped on women. I have a full-time job, I do the laundry, the food shopping, the cooking, and most of the childcare, i.e. doctor appointments, orthodontist visits, homework, logistics, party planning, etc. However, we cannot have it both ways. You cannot want control yet criticize the help. Or you cannot delegate but then dictate how said chore gets carried out. If you are evolved enough to understand this and recognize your own shortfalls you will understand at the end of the day the "he said, she said" gets you nowhere.

Can you laugh together? Have intimate conversations about the most vulnerable personal insecurities you have and still find your partner attractive?

If so, you have hit the pay dirt.

I have, but I need to continue to work on my own evolution.

SOMETIMES YOU FEEL LIKE A NUT, SOMETIMES YA DON'T

Each time, I think this memoir is done, I experience something that I want to share to help me dissipate my crazy. So as much as I have evolved, I have stayed the same. I just took a week-long vacation, which is the longest I have been away from my home since my honeymoon.

This was a real way for me to examine how far I have come, and what might just be impossible to change because of my DNA. As much as I try to rationalize with myself, and try to go with the flow, I find the challenge crippling at times. I can usually find a workaround but do not let my smile fool you. I battle daily demons, and I am going to reveal what it is like to be me.

We left for vacation on Tuesday. I had a discussion with myself for almost a week before I left and told myself that it would be okay to miss some exercise. In fact, I worked out seven days straight, so that I would feel even better about skipping some days while I was away. When I was going to bed on Monday night, I told Superman that there is a slight possibility that I might want to get up at 4 AM and ride my spin bike before we hit the road. He thought I was crazy, but I think he did not really think I would do it.

When I got up at four, he was on my tail and sort of glaring at me. He was, of course, concerned that I would cause us to have a late start (we anticipated a thirteen-hour car ride). I know exactly how long it takes me to get ready down to the minute. His worry was evidenced when he flickered the lights to give me a warning at 5 AM. As predicted, I was showered and dressed and ready to hit the road exactly on time. I just knew that getting one extra day of exercise in would make my disposition better.

On the road, it is often hard to find healthy food when you are at rest stops. I think we agreed upon pizza, which was a nice little treat. Knowing that I got that ride in allowed me to enjoy the gooey cheese. We got to the hotel, and I was very hungry and tired, but it was only around 3 PM. So, to stay awake, I had a Cliff Bar, and we went to an arcade. That was fun, and then we went out to dinner and back to the hotel. We broke the drive up into two days, so we still had seven hours to travel the next day until we arrived at our final destination.

We woke up and hit the road early. We were meeting up with thirty-six of Superman's cousin's, which was beyond fun. We got to our resort, and our room was not ready, so spontaneously we ended up going on an alpine slide that was exhilarating. We were all arriving at different times but met up for dinner at 7 PM. Whenever his family gets together, I am reminded of how lucky I am to have married into this bunch. I cannot believe the cohesiveness and love between such a large group. I did not want it to end.

That night we had a barbecue, and I was fine and relaxed. We went home, and the following day was Thanksgiving. I might as well reveal we were in Dollywood. I point this out because I am not sure if there are any vegetables in Tennessee. Couple that with a recall of romaine lettuce due to a countrywide e-Coli outbreak, and I was starting to get nervous that I would not be able to find anything that fit into my diet. Fried chicken, biscuits, and mashed potatoes were not regular staples at my house. I guess if I could have put them on top of a salad, then I would have felt better, but now lettuce was off limits too.

The good news is that I have been in the family long enough that they know I am a little odd around food. Everyone is aware that I work out in excess and that I am picky. For a good decade, they thought I was a vegan and Jewish, but that is a whole story in itself. So, knowing that we are going to be eating a lot, I decided to go for a run. I went to the gym, ran four miles, and then went to the breakfast buffet. This is a good time for me to bring up my next idiosyncrasy. If I work out, I need to do laundry immediately. So, before I book hotels, I always call to find out if there is a gym and guest laundry. I did three loads of laundry during the trip, which made me so happy. What is also notable is that Superman knows this about me, and when he finds the hotel, he looks too. He does not judge me (outwardly at least). This is another one of the many reasons I adore him. Of course, I made a friend in the laundry room, and Superman wondered if I invited her to dinner. She was an exerciser too, and we bonded over the food selections and the romaine recall. Instant friends.

The buffet had way too many choices, and I was overwhelmed. They had specialty breads, an omelet station, make your own doughnuts, make your own waffles, scones, bagels, quesadillas, oatmeal with brown sugar, and almonds, etc. I was able to make a middle of the road choice, but what I was worried about was the feast for Thanksgiving. Normally I host and trust me, I do not skimp on calories, but what I serve I give myself permission to eat. Not knowing the menu causes me anxiety. Another oddity that I was reminded of is I have trouble eating dinner for lunch. This is stupid considering science tells us that we burn calories better during the day when we are moving as compared to at night when we slow down. If I had to psychoanalyze myself, I think I would revert to my eating disordered days, when dinner would be my reward for making it through a full day of starving. With that mindset ingrained in my head for so long, the fear of eating a dinner sized meal earlier is that I would be hungry later but have consumed my quota for the day.

This weight obsession is a full-time job.

The meal ended up fine. Some angel made a salad with spring mix, and I had stuffing, turkey, of course, cranberry, and a biscuit, and I was good to go. I wish I could have let myself indulge in the desserts, but I could not do it. Regardless, the night was truly perfect. I knew the next day would be my favorite because we went on a six-mile hike uphill. Right up my alley. My Fitbit hit 20,000 steps. We went to a Christmas show at night. It was so much fun, but let me share the menu with you. Wait for it...

All you can eat, Southern fried chicken, clam chowder, biscuits, macaroni and cheese, ham, and mashed sweet potatoes. For dessert, there were huge apple turnovers. I texted my friend who has the constipation like I do, and said if you want to go, just eat the Dolly Parton diet and you will have no issues.

We got up the next morning and once again hit the road at the crack of dawn. It was a long trip, and when we arrived home, we were all exhausted. It was pouring rain, so we decided to order in. We got a take-out menu and before my very eyes was a salad in my beloved taco shell.

As I mentioned, I hate eating dinner for lunch, but it was three, and I decided that the oily shell was worth it. This salad was so good. I am guessing it was spring mix, but it resembled romaine, and let's just say I did not care. Here is when my demons come out. I ate every last drop, but I felt so badly about it, that I decided since the boys were just watching football anyway, that I would go to the gym and then do laundry. So, that is exactly what I did, and I was able to work through my guilt of eating the shell. I hate that I have to do that, but all I can say is that I accept my foibles, I know how to manage them, and I am not overdoing it, or purging, I am just a little nutty. We hung out and watched TV the rest of the night, woke up early, and now I am back to my comfortable abode.

I am not sharing this because I want everyone to think I am an odd duck, but I am sure each person reading this can relate to one part of this tale and my hope is that you recognize you are not alone. I get that comfort when someone, like my laundry room buddy acknowledges that she understands my thinking. Finding someone with the same thoughts legitimizes my feelings.

NOTE TO MY OLDER SELF

Since I am very happy at where I landed and would want the same exact outcome, I decided not to give advice to my younger self, but rather, to make sure that I make the most of the life I have left. I do hope I can find a way to not be as rigid as I have been in the past. It is not easy to teach an old dog new tricks, but as much as I make profound statements about letting go of the numbers, age, weight and all of those measures that dampen my mood, I am not sure how to detach. It is very logical and makes total sense when I advise other people to let go, but for some reason, I feel guilt and have a hard time doing the same for myself.

What concerns me is that I might not always be able to spin for ninety minutes or do Pilates on a reformer. I will continue as long as I can, but I think watching myself slow-down will be difficult. I also want to try not to compare myself to others. Nothing good comes from doing that, it is purely wasted energy. Ironically, the people I compare myself to are comparing themselves to me, which I have discovered after researching for this memoir. I want to make sure I cherish every moment with my son while he lives at home. He has taught me to embrace deep breathing. When he does not pick up his damn socks that are in every room, and the straw wrappers from his juice boxes, my blood pressure automatically rises. I do not love making two different dinners every night and finding Dorito bags in every pocket of clothing he owns, but I am going to miss watching him and his father roughhouse or watching him do his little *Fortnite* dances for me. I will miss listening to him, and his friends giggle.

I want to make sure that I cherish every day I get to spend with Superman. I cannot believe how I hit the husband jackpot. What does that mean? It does not mean we do equal chores, or he makes millions of dollars. It means I can tell him anything and everything without feeling judged. It means that we think the same thing or say the same line simultaneously because we are on the same page most of the time. It means we laugh and have the same intentions when raising our son. It means I feel loved, and I love him more than anything. I want to make sure that I will never take that for granted.

Sometimes going through a hard time makes you appreciate what you have. The threat of losing something that you take for granted is a hard pill to swallow. That happened for me, and since Superman and I had our challenge, there is truly not one day that I do not wake up and thank God that we made it through.

I want to continue to choose who I spend my time with mindfully. I have spent close to five decades doing the right thing without really thinking about how I feel. I have gone on several outings that I did not want to and had a bad time as a result. What I mean by this is doing things out of obligation rather than desire. What I used to consider fun is different from what I enjoy now. I do not like going out late anymore, and my interests have changed. So, when I automatically say yes, I almost immediately regret it. I want to think before I answer going forward. That does not mean that I will not attend baby showers, funerals, and hospital visits. There are certain things we all must do to show love, loyalty, and compassion.

I just mean that when someone asks me to go ziplining, I will now say no thank you. There was a time that might have sounded exciting. Now what comes to mind, is I need my legs, and what if I get hurt? This is just what happens as we age. We think about the consequences and decide if things are worth the risk. Everyone has a different threshold for risk. I think being a parent also changes your thinking. I chose to be a caretaker to a person I created. Therefore, I cannot always be selfish and think of only myself.

What do I anticipate? I wonder what it will feel like to not have to get up at 6 AM and make lunch, workout, do laundry, and prep dinner by 9 AM so I can work eight hours five days a week. I wonder what it will feel like to not have to chauffeur my son all over God's green earth, for a party, a baseball game, an outing, etc. I wonder if the emptiness I imagine I will feel when my son goes off to college will actually be as hard to handle as I envision.

I wonder if I will have to live in an assisted living unit like I watched my mother and mother-in-law acclimate to and ultimately suffer in. I wonder if I will be plagued with Alzheimer's. That may be the worst fear I have. I will not get tested until there is a cure.

Lastly, I wonder how I got so lucky to have my life. I think it is a combination of choices, luck and where you start from. All I can hope for is that I continue to be generous, inquisitive, and true to myself. I hope I will continue to share life's lessons and to remember to stop to smell the roses.

RUNAWAY THOUGHTS

I think what makes menopause harder than puberty, is that when you are young, you have the whole world ahead of you. Everything is up for grabs. At this stage, you have made a lot of decisions, but it feels like you are through a lot of the good stuff. I am trying so hard to remember, that I am at a point now, where I am financially in a good spot, have an established career, have a wonderful marriage and family and have a lot of autonomy when it comes to deciding what I do and do not want to do. I recall longing for a time where I did not have to do homework and take tests, and I did not want to go on yet another blind date and go through my story all over again only to be heartbroken.

It just seems to be going too fast. I recall when I was pregnant, worrying about what I would do when my son was at an age to do "boy things." I was petrified that I would not know how to keep him occupied and entertained. Now he is a teenager, and it went by in a blip. I am trying to savor the days, although not his teenager smell. That can speed right by. UGH, what is that?

Anyway, when I was writing each section, I was connecting the dots and trying to figure out what opportunities I was afforded by my paths. For example, when I decided to starve myself and become a high achiever, this steered me in a direction to hang out with similar friends wanting to attain the same things. As a result of this, I stumbled upon a love of exercise. I am sure, at first, it was solely as a means to an end. Somewhere along the way, I fell in love with exercising, the discipline, the kinesiology, the biology, and the ability to sculpt your body.

From that passion, I pursued several training certifications, which turned into a beautiful side career training clients, and now I have been doing it for twenty-five years. Not only has it been lucrative, but I have met some incredible people.

Wanting to share my love of exercise and how it freed me from my eating disorder, I started writing, for numerous fitness publications and eventually writing a fitness book.

This was an incredible opportunity that would not have presented itself if I did not take the road I chose. If I was not so self-conscious about my body, I might not have been so delayed in dating, and so standoffish. How would I have met my Prince Charming? It would not have happened. So, although I do not completely believe in fate, I do believe our choices impact which path we follow. I would choose the same path again if I would be assured of my life.

In that same vein, if I did not have the eating disorder, I would not have had the tools and understanding that helped save my marriage when Superman was in trouble. I related to the manipulation and the lies because I did the same thing with food that he did with alcohol. The pattern made sense to me, and we were able to get through it. In addition, I went around to high schools to share my story with other kids struggling with eating disorders, and really with anyone who could benefit from my story. I volunteered with the National Eating Disorder Associates of Long Island, raised tons of money and awareness for the disease. I did this to foster my own recovery. I could not imagine going through anorexia, coming out the other side, and not using the experience to help others. These are all opportunities that came out of a hard time.

I think if I did not date all those assholes, that I would not be able to appreciate the man that finally stole my heart. I did not realize that it is possible to have someone love you for who you are, without compromising your values until I experienced the opposite. I remember all the times I was waiting for phone calls or doing things that were not in my comfort zone for fear of being dumped. My husband called when he said he would and took an interest in figuring out what I wanted to do, and he made the effort. Of course, in return, I reciprocated, but it feels so much nicer when the appreciation is mutual. There is a difference between the butterflies that come from being insecure about where you stand and the ones that come from being in love.

The food thing, I have not resolved. I was going to write a fluffy profound statement that would be a lie. I have a love-hate relationship with food, which I will most likely have for the rest of my life. The elation I get from a good meal is almost odd. I love good food. I am scared of food, love it, and hate it. It has caused me health issues, energized me, made me hate, and love my body. Although I try to understand it and rationalize that its purpose is to fuel me, and provide me with the optimal health like high test gasoline, I cannot understand why there are so many unhealthy delicious options that we manufacture knowing the harm they can cause.

While I appreciate that my body allows me to move, and exercise and produce endorphins, I do not understand the betrayal I feel with my middle-aged weight gain and moving parts. By moving parts I mean my boobs going south and my abdomen extending north.

I try not to obsess, but I am failing. I think about how tight my clothes feel most of the day. While I am eating, I am trying not to feel guilty, and when I am depriving myself, I try not to be proud of my willpower, but this is who I am.

I would be remiss in minimizing certain situations that I have detailed. Being inappropriately touched, Anorexia, Alzheimer's, and Alcoholism are major serious struggles that really are a big deal. However, what I hope this memoir illustrates, is that we all are dealt some lemons. If you are able to step back and revisit when the emotions are not as raw, you can see how dealing with challenges head on can lead to growth and perhaps opportunities that you may not have been afforded otherwise. Independently there is not one of these hardships that I would want to go through again, but I do believe they brought me to my specific life, and I am very grateful to be here. With each challenge, my response is more thoughtful, and I am always reminded that how I choose to react will determine the outcome.

Thank God my husband allows me to fly my freak flag, because my constant obsession annoys the shit out of me, and I am the one in control (sort of).

While I do not think I look bad for my age in the mirror, I cannot help but realize that I am no longer the young one. I have been alive for half a century.

I think back to the time I got married, bought a house, got pregnant, and had so much in front of me. I was so excited about what lie ahead, but I was also anxious and unsure. While I do not like to think that all of the things I dreamed of as a kid are behind me, there is a certain peace knowing that I made it, and really, they all came true. There is still plenty to anticipate. My son going to high school and college, falling in love and starting a family of his own. Getting to a point where the majority of my time is not spent working and squeezing in the play time. I just cannot find a way to live in the now, without anticipating what is next. The great realization that I have come to is that I am so happy with my life that I want it to continue indefinitely. The caveat is, I want to feel good, maintain my health, and avoid aging.

I think because of what I witnessed having older parents, I am more cognizant of the perils of old age and watching your body betray you. As a person who gets so much fulfillment from movement, I dread losing my capacity to be in command of my body. In the recesses of my mind, I do worry that I will be afflicted with

Alzheimer's like my mother and uncle. The only saving grace, sorry Superman, is that I will not really remember what is happening, which could be the only way for someone with my control issues to survive. When I told Superman that he should be prepared to drug me and put me out of my misery if he saw a decline in my mental state, he hopped right on that bandwagon.

I wish time would slow down, but I know that is not realistic. This is what I am trying to figure out, and I am determined to make some peace with it, so I do not waste any precious time.

ACKNOWLEDGEMENTS

As I was going through all of the people I wanted to thank, I had a flashback to high school, my wedding, my baby shower, and I am reminded that inadvertently I am going to leave someone out by mistake, and they are going to be mad at me. I caution that person that there could be a part two, and if you are resentful, I may use you in a chapter.

Seriously, so many people were instrumental in helping me share my vulnerabilities and encouraged me that I will still have friends even though I polluted Penn Station.

Laurie Jackel, who listened to every chapter more than once, who called me to check on the progress of my work. Sally Hepworth, who was at my house and wanted me to work on another book I had started entitled "Don't Waste My Eggs." Superman does not need to know about my eggs.

Fiona Davis, who read my work and praised it. I have such respect and admiration for her writing, this kept me encouraged while I was looking for a publisher. My sister, Wendy Valentino, who relived many of the moments with my parents and appreciated some of the endearing weird moments of our upbringing. Lisa Smith, who offered her time and her expertise, no matter where she was traveling and promoting her own book. She was beyond generous with her time and support.

Michelle Chernack, who I love beyond belief, for the goodness that emanates from her, and the endless support she brings to our friendship.

Laurie Chittenden, who is the best editor in the world. I love her as a person and a talent. I could not have done it without her.

Lastly to Keith and Luke Condon, my heart.

NOTE FROM THE AUTHOR

Word-of-mouth is crucial for any author to succeed. If you enjoyed the book, please leave a review online—anywhere you are able. Even if it's just a sentence or two. It would make all the difference and would be very much appreciated.

Thanks!
Laurie

ABOUT THE AUTHOR

Laurie Condon has been writing articles and blogs for two decades. Most of them focus on Fitness, and self- care. They have appeared in *Ms. Fitness, Personal Fitness Professional, Health Products Business, Club Industry, The Nutritious Life Studio and S-Life Magazine.* She self-published a book entitled *Keeping Fit on The Run*, which was purchased by a company for their salespeople. She lives on Long Island with her husband and their son.

Thank you so much for reading one of our **Self-Help/Personal Growth** books. If you enjoyed the experience, please check out our recommended title for your next great read!

This Side Up by Amy Mangan

AMY MANGAN

This Side Up

The Road to a Renovated Life

A Memoir

"A story of a fighter and fixer. An inspiration to us all."

"*This Side Up* will leave you feeling relieved, not alone, hopeful, and grateful for a friend and writer like Amy Mangan who inspires us to reframe our let downs, have some laughs, and embrace life with all of its beautiful unexpected messes." –Stacy Strazis, former producer *The Oprah Winfrey Show* and *CNN*

CPSIA information can be obtained
at www.ICGtesting.com
Printed in the USA
FSHW020547021219
64461FS